THE FOUR KINGDOMS OF NATIVE'S POINT

Clayton Johnson

New Harbor Press

RAPID CITY, SD

Johnson/New Harbor Press
1601 Mt. Rushmore Rd, Ste 3288
Rapid City, SD 57701
NewHarborPress.com

Publisher's Note: This is a work of fiction. Names, characters, places, and incidents are a product of the author's imagination. Locales and public names are sometimes used for atmospheric purposes. Any resemblance to actual people, living or dead, or to businesses, companies, events, institutions, or locales is completely coincidental.

Ordering Information:
Quantity sales. Special discounts are available on quantity purchases by corporations, associations, and others. For details, contact the "Special Sales Department" at the address above.

The Four Kingdom's of Native's Point/Clayton Johnson. -- 1st ed.
ISBN 978-1-63357-285-0

Prologue

M any years ago, the kingdom of Autem came to the new land. Being a kingdom so big in numbers, they had the military power to take control of the land. None of the other three major kingdoms in the land, Gresham, Nalaryia, and Leonkam, could hope to challenge Autem and take the land back.

Alone that is. Led by Leonkam, the three kingdoms stood together and rebelled to end the reign of Autem in the new land. Knowing they were beat, Autem signed a peace treaty. This allied the four kingdoms and together they made a force that would stand up to any outsiders that would look to conquer the land. They have ruled together dominantly for many years. This is where our story begins.

RICHARD

I am a Hayward. From a long line of Haywards, actually. My family has been the first family of Gresham for generations. My uncle ruled as king during the war against Autem, but that was a long time ago now. Since then, he has passed on and now Gresham's new king is his son, my cousin Timothy.

He is far too young to wear the crown. In fact, without the help of my father guiding him, I doubt the kingdom would last a week. My father Bruce is the military general and adviser to King Timothy. In short, he runs the show. I have been training under my father all my life. As a member of the royal family from birth I was expected to have daily swordsmanship training as well as learning the ins and outs of politics between the kingdoms . . . ugh, a subject that always bored me. I did love the competition of sword fighting, but as I got older and the reality that winning a sword fight meant someone would most likely lose their life set in, it just wasn't as much fun.

Speaking of which, I'm late for today's training. Time to throw on the armor and get on with the day, I guess. I begin the process of strapping up my steel set with green cloth draped over the neck, the color of Gresham. Helmet in my hand I rush down the stairs from my quarters. I cut through the castle's kitchens, it's the fastest way to the yard. I know I'm running late but it smells so good I wonder if I have time for a quick breakfast.

I push through and make it to the yard. A lot of bodies occupying it at the moment, the whole army in fact, other than those on guard duty. And standing in front of them all, my father. Everyone else is hard at work already. Nothing else to do but walk up to my dad and try to explain why I'm late, if I even get the chance.

"Son," my dad says upon seeing me. I try to be quick with my response before the lecture I'm sure is coming begins.

"Father, I have a great excuse for why I'm late . . . again . . . it's a funny story actually! You're going to laugh."

"Oh, no need, my boy," he said with a grin on his face, "but, as you can see, everyone else already has a sparring partner for the day . . . looks like you'll be paired up with Ridge."

Well, if I was hoping for a light day, it looks like I'm out of luck. Ridge, who I have the unfortunate obligation to train with for the day, is by far the biggest man in our army. The top of his bald head stands just short of seven feet tall, and he is seemingly wide as a bull. Most men would probably be scared of him. But not me, I know what I'm capable of.

I turn and face Ridge. "Draw your sword, best we get to it," I say.

He does just that and draws. After a brief moment, he charges in. Not surprisingly, a guy his size is used to being the strongest in most battles. He's expecting his opponent to back up in fear, but I won't play his game. I stand my ground. While I'm not nearly as big as him, I would like to think I'm a pretty strong guy, let's hope I'm strong enough block this strike. Our blades hit hard. He put a lot into that swing. With any luck I can get him to gas himself out. To do that I'm going to want to hurt his pride. Attacking straight on is a no go but I bet with some good timing I can knock him off his feet. I swing high and intentionally slow, expecting a counterstrike. Ridge ducks swiftly and lunges forward at me. Just in time, I roll off. Avoiding his blade, I quickly place my foot behind his heel. I take my forearm and shove it in his chest with a healthy amount of force behind it. That knocks him off his feet and puts him on his ass.

"Shame," I say, "I was hoping for more of a challenge." He hops up just as fast as he fell, just as I knew he would. He looks angrier this time so my words of encouragement must have worked. He raises his blade and I takes a deep breath getting ready to weather the storm. He starts his attack. Though it's not easy, I put all I have into blocking strike after strike until, finally, Ridge lets up. I'm breathing hard but it's easy to tell he's more tired than I am. Time to finish this. I swing high and Ridge reacts by putting his sword over his head to block it. However, a well-timed knee to his gut takes out what little air he had left and puts him to his knee.

"Okay, okay . . . You win, I yield," said Ridge gasping for a breath. Not a bad fight after all. I reach out my hand to help him up. After all, there's no hard feelings, it's just training.

"Good, good." I hear my father's voice. "You have a natural strategic mind. Now if you would put more effort into being someone these men can respect, it would get you much farther when they are under your command." As if I needed to be reminded that after my father I am next in line to serve. As general, nonetheless, a job that I don't even know if I want. The thought of men's lives hanging on the choices I make is a lot of pressure to say the least. But that's something I won't have to worry about for a long while. I mean I am just now twenty-two years old. Not to mention we're at peace times and, even if we got attacked, the combined force of the four kingdoms makes even the strongest armies look weak. No, my dad will be general for a long while.

Still, it's not hard to see how similar my father and I are, and he seems to love the gig. We even look alike. We have the same light brown hair, blue eyes, and are of the same build. Both around a height a couple inches away from six feet, with a more broad base to our frames. He does however have a goatee growing in that I am not a fan of.

"It's time you take on more responsibly," he says. "As you know, I attend the meeting with the other three kingdoms in place of Timothy. But this time, I am choosing to send you instead. Get ready for your trip to Leonkam."

ALISTAIR

"Four kings in charge of one land. Have you ever heard of such a bloody thing?" I yell out in my throne room to anyone who will listen. Everyone in the room should listen, I am their king after all. When I start a rant, they better pay attention like their lives depend on it. After all, it very well could.

"Why can't the whole world follow the same laws as Leonkam? After all, do you think I have this crown sit atop my head because lesser men signed a paper declaring me their king? No! I am your king because not a single one of you would dare try to take this crown off me. I am the strongest, so I am your leader. This has been the Leonkam way for all of time."

In the coming days, speakers from the other three kingdoms will be here to meet with me, Alistair Godwin. At least it is my kingdom's turn to host the meeting. It's bad enough I have to break bread with men I know to be inferior but having to leave Leonkam would be the rotten cherry on top. I suppose this is not without its rewards, however. After all, as a king I am forced to think of my people. They are the reason I agreed to peace. Doing what is in my people's best interest will always be a no brainer. Even if it means playing nice with the filth from Autem.

"Sir, there is a local woman at the castle door requesting a word with you. Should I tell her to leave?"

The man talking is a knight from my guard named Steven. I know him well as I've taken the time to know every man in my guard well.

"No, send her in. I have little else occupying me at the moment," I say. With a nod Steven goes to retrieve the woman. I stare down the long hall of my throne room watching as the door opens at the end. Then walks in this woman who looks as if she had been battling longer than I. Her red ratty dress went down to her old shoes that had a spilt at the sole. Her hair was blonde and matted.

"So?" I say, "What have you come to request of me today?"

"Food, my king," she said with a quiver in her voice.

"Yet you appear to have no handicap. Why is it you must ask me for food instead of working for it yourself?"

"My king, I clean the marketplace for what little coin I have. This request is not for me, but for my child. I buy food for him and try to keep a roof over his head, but I can't afford much . . . and he has grown so skinny."

"I see . . . you are a mother doing the job of both a mother and a father." Normally, I would rant. I would tell her this kingdom is a place where you earn what you get. A beautiful place where you are as successful as how hard you're willing to work. But none of that applies here; this woman's hard work is put toward making sure her child is successful. That should be rewarded. Then again maybe I am just getting softer with age as I am now a man nearing his fifties.

"You make your kingdom proud. People with drive to take care of their own like you have is why this kingdom is great . . . Sir Steven, see to it that a bore is delivered to this woman."

"Thank you! I am forever grateful, my king."

With a nod, I send her on her way. I think I did the right thing. As she's walking out, I smell a faint scent of smoke. From outside the window, clear as ever, I can see the cause. Leonkam's stables up in flames . . . .

NEAL

Crickets. The sound is loud as ever, come nightfall here in Nalaryia. I love that sound, it's when I do my best work. Tonight, I am in the bushes staring at the good-sized hut of a well-off man named Roman Cooper. Roman decided that even though he could afford it, he was going to rob a local merchant. Said the man looked at him wrong. Unluckily for him, I am an enforcer of the law here in Nalaryia, so I'm paying him a visit this fine evening. I blend in well. My armor is almost all black, other than the blue shoulder pads as to represent the color of Nalaryia.

Tonight's visit is long overdue for Roman. You see, in addition to being just an all-around bad guy, Roman is a slave owner, a horrible practice that he gets away with due to the laws of our kingdom. You see, twenty years ago Nalaryia passed a law that ended slavery as a request from the King of Gresham at the time. The deal was made to keep the peace. But the King of Nalaryia decided to puff his chest out. So, the law was made that all existing slaves remain, however, no citizen of the kingdom would be born into slavery from that point on.

Which explains why I have such a vested interest in people like Roman. I wait for them to slip up and break the law, then I go after them and in the end people go free.

Alright, I've been staking this place out for hours and, as far as I can tell, he's alone. Seems like his slaves are asleep in his small stable. Time to move in. Easy enough to slip in the back window. Sneaking through this guy's home, watching every step. I can't take the risk of him running.

Alright. He should be sleeping. All I need to do is open his wooden bedroom door. Here's to hoping the door doesn't squeak. I open it as slowly as possible . . . all clear and I'm in. He's in bed sleeping all right. The closest exit is a window to the right of the bed. Better stand in front of it to block his escape. He'll be easier to catch if he runs for the door, because he'd never make it there in time. After all, I am known as "the fastest sword in the land" for a reason. Alright, here goes nothing.

I draw my sword and point it at him. "Roman Cooper!" I loudly announce. His eyes dart open and a look of confusion covers his face.

"I find you guilty of assault and robbery!" I say.

"What the hell are you doing breaking into my hut! You must know who I am!"

"I know alright! You're slave-owning trash."

"Ah. I understand now, there's been talk of someone going after the remaining slave owners. Don't think I don't know who you are. 'The fastest sword in the land.'

What did you think was going to happen here? I have well enough money to get out of jail, and I'll just come right back to my slaves, and YOU. Well, I'll come back to your head hanging ON MY WALL . . . Neal Greyson," he spits.

His smug look lets me know he truly believes he's in no danger.

"That may be true . . . but you're not going to jail."

I raise my sword and the smug look leaves his face.

"What? No! you can't!"

"I can. After all, you attacked me. I was just here to make an arrest. At least, that's how everyone will remember it."

"I have money . . . I'll give it to you . . . as much as you want!"

Funny how fast a tune can change when a man has his back against a wall. With one swift motion, I bring down my sword . . . .

SAMUEL

"Prince Samuel, your father King Wallace is requesting you," my most trusted servant Edward said to me. "Well," I say, "then let's not keep him waiting." After all, I have already gotten everything ready for my trip to Leonkam. I am wearing my armor fit for a prince. The finest silver set with stainless cape hung at the shoulders, it would be impossible for someone to treat me with disrespect wearing a set that looks this good, and that includes my father.

We step out of my quarters and into the long, tall hallway of our great castle. The most beautiful castle between the four kingdoms, built on the backs of the natives when our great nation of Autem first settled here and had full control of the land. I only wish I were old enough before the war to enjoy that time. However, I was just a boy. The war ended around twenty years ago and I am just now twenty-six. It took three other kingdoms together to stand up to us. Seems pretty clear to me that Autem is the strongest by far of the four kingdoms and we treat the others like equals. WHY? I don't think I'll ever understand.

"You know your father's condition . . . it's getting worse. You should make an effort to connect with him. Soon you may not have the chance to. Despite what you believe, you father does love you," Edward tells me. If he was anyone else, I would tell him to keep his opinion to himself. But Edward has been in my service all my life and he has always looked out for me.

"Love?" I say, "So is love the reason that even though he has been on bed rest and can't even sit in his throne he refuses to give me the crown?!" Edward doesn't answer. He knows he won't change my way of thinking. The expression on his face makes him look very unsettled. However, this makes me wonder just how rough of shape my father really is in. The remainder of the walk is quiet. When we finally get to my father's quarters, Edward gives me a look that tells me what I need to know. A "get ready" kind of look.

I open the door. This room is much bigger than any other quarters in the keep. The nice, clean, wood floors and stone walls are washed every day. There, my dear old dad lays in his bed. All but his head under covers. Edward was right, he doesn't look good. His old, wrinkled face on his light brown skin, and a hat of pure white hair on top.

It looks like we're alone. He must have sent the maids away.

"Father . . . you asked for me," I say. He looks up to see me.

"My son. My only son . . . " he said. "I just wanted to check in on you before you left for the meeting in Leonkam."

"I am fine, father . . . but you know, it may help those low lives to better know who's in charge if I walk in wearing a crown?"

"Son, we've talked about this."

"What are we waiting for?! You are not getting any better. Why would you rather be in the ground than see me be king."

"BECAUSE YOU'RE NOT FIT TO RULE!" my father yelled. I didn't know what to say. How dare he? I should have raised my voice, but I couldn't get any words out. I just need time to let what he said sink in. He starts to speak again, "I do love you, my son, but I would die before I gave the crown to a man that is too angry and self-absorbed to lead our great people in the right direction." Angry and self-absorbed? How could I not be? I KNOW I am next in line to rule the strongest nation and I am forced put myself on the same shelf as the common folk.

"Well then," I say, "I guess it's a good thing you don't have a lot of time left." I turn and exit the room. I find myself surprised at how much those words hurt me to say. I do want to be king, but I hope he knows I don't really want him dead. I look up to see an old friend of mine wandering the halls. Her name is May Duchsen. She has a personality that shines even above her looks. In fact, if I had just a little more of her kindness in me, my father may have made me king.

Her bright green eyes are prominent on her caramel skin and her long black hair is done perfectly. She was born to a high-end family and has since worked her way up to be on the advisory board of the king.

"Good morning, May," I say. "Can I expect your company on the way to Leonkam?" We grew up together but have drifted in our adult lives. I would much enjoy reconnecting.

"But of course," she says. "After all, someone has to advise you against declaring war."

"You know, being a pacifist was never one of my strengths."

"You're right," she laughs, "I can recall more than one fight in the school yard growing up."

"Ha. It was hardly fair. As prince I was trained in all aspects of fighting on the daily."

"I can only hope you play nicer with the other kings at the meeting tomorrow. It's about time to head that way, isn't it?" I hold out my arm, "Shall we?" I escort her to our convoy.

As you can imagine with the meeting holding four people of power in one spot, the utmost of protection is needed. Each visiting kingdom is to bring forth one of their guards. We travel in unmarked convoys as not to make a show of it. It's better that no one knows that a big chunk of the guard is leaving the kingdom. We travel through the night and arrive by morning. I made small talk with May for a few hours, until it was decided I should get some rest for what the following day would bring. Upon opening my eyes from my sleep, we had arrived at Leonkam's gate. We, the convoy, go through the dirt streets. The citizens, many of which have dirt-covered clothing, stare at us as we go by. They are hard-working people. The guards of the city keep a very close eye on us, due to the history between our nations, I'm sure. All in uniform, they wear chainmail around their torso and head with a red tunic overtop. Iron forearm plates, and more iron armor on the legs. Most wear great swords or spears on their backs.

When we reach the castle with guards by our side, I walk May inside. When we enter the room in which we hold the meeting, I see a large round table in the center. Seems that Alistair and King Adonjay from Nalaryia have not arrived yet. It does look like the Gresham representative is here. A young man that I have never seen before, he looks nervous and out of place. "You there," I say, "What's your name?"

He looks over and responds. "I am Richard Hayward from Gresham."

"Bad enough your boy king does not show up himself, but now your general, Bruce, sends someone in his place."

"Bruce is my father. I am next up to command the Gresham army."

"You think you have a place here because you share a name with men of greater power then yourself . . . you don't belong here." I don't entertain him long enough to

see his reaction to what I just told him. I just turn, walk
to the table, and take my seat.

RICHARD

I hope that's not telling of how the rest of this meeting is going to go. Still, maybe he has a point. I am no one special. Hell, I don't even wear armor to befit a commander. Just like holding the title of general, that's a privilege only my father has. I know one day I will wear that commander armor and run our army. As for as I know, however, whether it's from what I wear, to my rank, I am nobody important. Why did my dad think these people would treat me any different than what I am?

"I apologize for Prince Samuel," I hear a soft female voice tell me. "He has a habit of coming off a touch rude."

"Old habits die hard, I guess," I respond jokingly. With a slight chuckle, she introduces herself. "I am May Duchsen, adviser to the throne of Autem. Pleased to meet you."

"Richard Hayward of Gresham. Your kind attitude has been out of the ordinary so far this trip."

"You'll grow stronger for it. I'm sure Gresham sends only the most capable to these things. Your father Bruce is one of the only men here they all seem to respect. If he sent you, you must be quite honorable." Looks as if I'm in for yet another trail of trying to live up to the exceptions set by my father. "Time will tell," I say to her then I turn to go take my seat at the table.

There is an awkward silence as Prince Samuel and I are the only two at the table right now. Then, I see the door open, and through it walks in King Adonjay of Nalaryia. He is dressed in the finest robes and has a crown on his head. What their kingdom lacks in size, they make up for in wealth. His old, wrinkled face looks snaky as ever. Behind him walks his top soldier. Wearing black armor with blue shoulder pads with a long light-weight sword strapped to his side, he has ginger hair and a beard to match. I hear some Leonkam guards whis-pering in the background, "Watch what you say around that one. That's Neal Greyson, the fastest swordsman in the land." Adonjay takes his seat and Neal stands behind him. There is just one seat left at the round table to fill.

Without much more time lost, Alistair Godwin en-ters the room with his guard Sir Steven. I've seen him at meetings in my kingdom before, and every time his size alarms me. Nearing in on six-and-a-half-foot tall with a very wide, muscular frame, and always carrying his large greatsword on his back. Alistair takes his seat, and his guard stands behind him.

"Seems we're all here," Samuel says, "sooner we get to business, the sooner we get done." Alistair sends over a dirty look and says, "I couldn't agree more."

"Allow me to kick off the show," said King Adonjay, "As you know, we outlawed new slave owners when we agreed to peace after the war. However, due to recent events, some of our existing owners have been . . . well, they are not in the picture anymore. Much of our wealth is made on the backs of our slaves. I am requesting today that we change the law so that we may again have more slaves to uplift our economy." Behind him, I see Neal grind his teeth.

"Nalaryia's wealth benefits us all. If a few more of the lower class have to be subject to free labor, it's a small price to pay," said Samuel. I swear he doesn't think before he opens his mouth. "You're joking," I say, "taking any citizen's free will is too much of a price to pay, I would argue. These were my uncle's terms when he lived, and you agreed to them . . . nothing changes."

Adonjay rises his eyebrow, "So, I see we let just anyone sit at this table now . . . whatever the case, Alistair, it seems you have the deciding vote." As Alistair goes to speak, I interrupt, "No, you misunderstand. There is no vote. You will be paying your labors from now on." A look around the table lets me know the others think I overstepped my bounds. Alistair looks partially angry, must not like being cut off. He looks like he's about to begin his rant. "I agree with the lad." He said to my surprise. King Adonjay hangs his head.

"Thank you for agreeing, King Alistair," I say.

"Not so fast, boy. You come in here and sit at a table of men who hold real power, and you think you can make demands . . . you know during the war, your uncle wanted to find every way to make peace without battle.

Your people talk about wanting freedom but aren't willing to fight for it. You're cowardly, just like your uncle." Just when I was beginning to think everyone here wasn't out to get me. They clearly see my being here as an insult. Throwing insults on my name is one thing but insulting my kingdom and even my family, my late uncle nonetheless, boils my blood.

I hold my tongue so I don't say anything to hurt our kingdom's relationship, even though I would very much like to speak out. At least Adonjay didn't get his way and gain more slaves. King Godwin smirks like he just put me in my place. He starts to speak, "Now, to other matters. My stables were burnt to the ground last night. Horses and a stable boy burnt along with it. This was no accident. Men dressed all in black were seen fleeing the scene."

Samuel answers, "Hmm. We'll be on the lookout for this stable arson. Thank you for bringing this to our attention."

"Funny. Without horses, my troops would be at a disadvantage.

And this happens right before you waltz in here with a big chunk of guard."

"You can't be suggesting I had something to do with this?"

"Not at all. We are agreed to peace, of course. I'm simply acknowledging that Autem has things to gain from the fall of Leonkam."

"Oh, that is rich . . ." Samuel rants and the two bicker for some time. Alistair does have a point. It's no secret that Leonkam and Autem have been at odds since the war. After a while the argument ends, and the meeting comes to a close. We agree to let Alistair know if we hear anything about who burnt down his stables. All of us flood out of the castle and into the streets. Most of the buildings are made of stone out here. It figures, because Leonkam is the farthest kingdom to the east in the mountains. The land we all live is referred to as Native's Point and connects to the sea. Autem is farthest south in the beaches at the point, northwest is Nalaryia in the grasslands, and southwest is Gresham is the heart of the forest, meaning it's a long trip home.

As I am about to board my convoy, I hear the screams of a woman calling for help. I turn to see the source and it is an elderly woman dressed in cheaply made cloth. Her cries for help are ignored by everyone walking by. "Why am I so busy that I can't take time out to assist the elderly?" I think to myself. Admittedly, not something I would always do, but seeing people walk by as if they're all too busy is making me feel convicted over it.

I approach her, but before I can say a word, she grabs my arm. "Please, sir, I need your help."

"What's happened?" I answer.

"They've taken it from me!"

"Whoa, slow down, just explain to me what's going on and I will see if I can help."

"It's a necklace, but more than that, it's been in my family for quite a long time. It gets passed down through the men of my family. Most recently it belonged to my husband. He had intended to give it to our son. They both fought in the war . . . but . . ." her voice begins to shake, "Neither of them came home." She tells me.

Widows seem to be a common trend of Leonkam. Maybe if Alistair had taken the advice of my uncle during the war, things would be different. She continues, "I now am alone . . . I try the best I can to pay the high tax of our city . . . but I was not able to gather enough coin to do so. My home was searched and the necklace, being the only thing I have of value, was taken from me as payment." This woman has been through enough. She is completely alone and Leonkam wants more from her. Alistair thinks this is a place where hard work will achieve dreams, but hard-earned coin is taken from them with high tax. Additionally, hard work can't bring back a fallen son.

I am sure this necklace means as much to her as she says it does. I think back to my cousin Timothy who never goes anywhere without his father's sword. They hold on tight to the objects because it's a little piece of a loved one they've lost.

"Do you have any idea of where the necklace is now?" I ask.

"That's why I'm yelling for help. As of now, it should still be with the guards that took it, in the barracks. If we wait any longer, it will be moved to the treasury and impossible to get back."

"Won't the barracks be loaded with guards?"

"Normally, yes, but with the meeting today they will all be around the keep on watch. It will be an easy steal." She says this to me with a glimmer of hope in her eyes.

I don't know if it had more to do with me feeling bad for her, or maybe it's just because I want to get back at Alistair for insulting my family, but I look over to the lead wagon of my convoy and instruct them to wait outside the city. If things go south, I may have to leave in a hurry.

I tell this woman to wait for my return. I start my walk to the guard barracks. The way she made it sound, it should be as simple as walking in and grabbing the necklace. I put my helmet on. There is nothing distinguishing about my armor, and it will be less to answer for if it's just a random Gresham soldier that gets seen stealing here than a Hayward himself.

Upon reaching the barracks, I notice the doorway is unguarded. "Maybe this will be as easy as I hoped," I think to myself. I do a quick scan, and when the coast is clear I walk in. To my surprise, the old lady was right. It's a completely empty room of beds and foot chests. Not wanting to spend any unnecessary time here, I start going through the foot chests as fast as possible.

Opening almost all of them, and still nothing. Just when I think I'm out of luck, I am able to lay my eyes on it in one of the last chests. I can see why her family has kept it so long. It's a beautiful gold necklace with a big red ruby. As I am admiring it, I hear the creaking of the door. I let out a sigh, knowing that I have missed my clean getaway. I turn to look to see Sir Steven, one of Alistair's guards, from the meeting looking back at me with a confused look on his face. "What are you doing here, soldier?" he asks. I don't say anything in fear that he would recognize my voice. He looks at me, then at the necklace in my hand, and his eyes widen. "THIEF!" he yells and draws his sword. There are no guards around to hear him, but I know I'll have to fight my way out of here. I draw my sword. Sword in hand, he rushes over. I rise to block and our blades meet. We each push against each other until we break low but he's able to catch me with an elbow to the helmet with his sword hand on the way out. I swing back in anger. He blocks, pushes me off, and puts the flat of his sword in my stomach knocking the wind out of me. Also letting me know he's not trying to kill me. He's good . . . but he's not wearing a helmet so I'll see what I can do with that. I know I'm not going to kill him so taking this fight to the ground is my best chance. I pull back my sword as far as I can and throw it with all I have in the direction of his head.

I know I said I wasn't trying to kill him but trust me, a swordsman like him will be ready to block it. It was thrown only as a distraction. He blocks it, as I thought, but while he's busy with that, I dive at his legs with a power double leg takedown driving him to the floor. I came at him with enough force that he drops his sword.

He's scrambling to get up, hitting me with body shots in the ribs. I make sure to get him back with a few of my own. He's getting angrier every second he's down. In a desperate attempt to get to his feet, he rolls to try and stand up, giving me his back. Without a helmet, it's all too easy to get to his neck. I sink in a deep choke as he struggles. It gets tighter and tighter. He fights as long as he can but, soon enough, out he goes.

I know he'll be fine, and he'll wake up soon, so I grab my sword and the necklace and head out in a hurry. I walk fast, keeping my head down, until I get all the way back to the old woman. "Here," I say, giving her the necklace. "I know this doesn't bring them back, but it is all I can do."

She looks up at me as if she's about to cry. It's clear to her this necklace is much more than just a piece jewelry. She simply says, "Your kindness will not be forgotten." On that note, I turn and leave. I wish there to be hopeful days ahead for her, as well as hoping that little stunt doesn't get me in any unwanted trouble with Alistair . . . I guess only time will tell.

ALISTAIR

G lad that's over. Now to have a little fun, I always plan a hunt after one of those dreaded meetings. I find it to be a great way to blow off steam and relax a little. I head to my quarters to get ready. It's sure to be a good one, as we're spear hunting rams in the nearby mountains. A few of my men are meant to meet me by the keep's doors to join me.

The nerve of that Hayward boy making demands like he's a real player in this game. Plus, the more I talk to Prince Samuel the more I know it will be havoc in Autem when he takes the crown. That's when the real game for Native's Point will start. This peace that we agreed to is a sham, that is becoming more and more clear by the day. These boys moving into power have the potential to bring war to my doorstep. Striking first would be the smartest thing to do, but then it would be three against one.

"My king! I have news!" I turn to see one of my castle's guard rushing towards me. "What's happened?" I say.

"It's Steven, sir. He was found in a bad way; says he was attacked in the guard barracks by a Gresham solider."

"Where is he now? I need to hear his full story."

"We figured as much, sir. He's down in the throne room waiting for you."

I turn and head that way as a million thoughts run through my head. First, the arson of our stables, now an attack on one of my knights. Still, I have yet to know the motive for the fight with Steven, but it's becoming hard to not think that someone isn't out to hurt Leonkam. After all, if we're out of the way, taking sole control of Native's Point would be that much easier. Now, with news of Steven's fight, Gresham is beginning to look the part of a prime suspect. Maybe king Timothy's bravery has been brought on from a life of privilege. Or more likely that cousin of his, Richard, is in his ear, feeding him a fantasy of Timothy being king of all four kingdoms. Little weakling probably thinks that if a war goes well in Gresham's favor, he'll end up with a castle of his own. I walk into the throne room to see Steven there looking a little worse for wear.

"Tell me exactly what happened." I say sternly. I can tell he's nervous to tell me of his defeat. He should be. He begins to talk, "After the meeting, I went back to the barracks to prepare for our ram hunt, my king. That's when I saw a Gresham soldier looting our chests! I can't put my finger on why, though. I've already instructed the men to go and report anything missing from there chest."

"That doesn't matter." I say, "The reason that man broke in was just to see if he could. If us and Gresham were ever at odds, they now know they can get into our guard barracks. Most likely to kill men in their sleep, should they find a way into the city."

"My king, I'm sorry. I should have stopped him."

"Yes, you should have . . . but we can't change the past, we can only prepare for what's to come. I suggest you go train, to insure you don't fail me again." Make no mistake, peace is at the end of its rope, and the game for Native's Point has already started.

NEAL

O ur convoy has started our trip west back to Nalaryia.
It's a grim trip back as I am forced to spend it alone
in a closed carriage with King Adonjay. Just he and I, all
the way through the forest of Gresham, until we reach
the grasslands of our home. With any luck, I'll be able to
ride out this trip in peace and quiet.

"Well, that could have gone better." Adonjay starts
talking as my hope of an uneventful trip disappears.
"Nevertheless," he continues, "we'll get what we want.
We're one vote away and that Hayward boy is so green
he doesn't know how badly he needs our money. Deep
down, they all know that us keeping wealth off slaves'
backs is best for everyone. The second conflict comes,
they need more swords, more arrows, more food."

He makes me sick. Could he sound any more like a
man with a sense of superiority? "Writings talk about
how God split the sea so that Moses could walk slaves to
freedom. Maybe he will have justice done in Nalaryia as
well." I say coming back at him. By the look on his face,
he's not happy I choose to disagree with him. He begins
to speak, "Ah, you and your Christian faith. May I ask
where your god was when you yourself were sold into

slavery? I'd imagine you were quite angry at him when your mother, also a slave, was no longer worth what it cost to keep her fed."

It's true. I am a slave. My mother and I were sold into it when I was just a boy. So, you can see why I have such a hate for slaving. Unfortunately, my mother grew old and, for a slave in Nalaryia, that's basically a death sentence. They don't kill you, but they exile you outside of the city walls. Already starving, the chances of making it to Gresham without meeting your end is unlikely. I never did find out what happened to her, but I think about her every day. I was a sneaky kid then, so after our owner sent her to die on the road, I slipped into his room for revenge. I know it sounds awful that I would do that at such a young age, but I was heartbroken. I did what I did and made sure he paid for what happened to my mom. From that point on I was given the choice of death or to be a personal slave to the king. He put my stealth skills to use and kept me climbing the ranks of his army until I got to the top. I think he liked the idea of someone in command being his personal dog.

"My mother may still have victory in heaven," I say while shooting him a stern look, "but you are going to burn. A fate I wouldn't wish on anyone, though we all deserve it."

"Remember who you're talking to, slave! You can dream of the afterlife while you sleep, but while you are awake, you belong to ME."

I sit back in my seat and let the conversation die out and we both silently ride in anger.

As I sit back, undistracted, I realize that at some point in our argument, our wagon stopped moving. I become uneasy because I know we're nowhere near our destination. Then, Adonjay makes a face, as if he is just noticing our stop as well.

"Stay here and listen carefully," I tell him. I start to slowly open the door, sword in hand. Peeking my head out, I look behind us, and see that we have somehow separated from the other wagons. I look forward to the driver, and though he's wearing the blue of our kingdom, I don't recognize him. "Driver! What's happened? Where are we?" I yell to him. He turns very slowly to face me, and I become sure I have never seen this man before. He turns his face into a smile as I hear the whistling of arrows through the wind. One of them crashes into my shoulder but thankfully my armor slows it, so it does little to hurt me.

I see men with bows and swords rushing us from the trees, way too many to fight. "MY KING!" I yell. "We have to run!" Two men reach us as Adonjay is getting out. I swipe at the first man's leg after ducking his swing at my head. He drops to a knee. I raise quickly to kick him into the man behind him. With no time to lose, the king and I flee into the woods, with men hot on our heels.

SAMUEL

Not many things are better than the smell of Autem air after going to one of those awful meetings. Our wagons ride in through the city walls. "You know something, May? I wish I did burn down those stables. That Alistair needs to be reminded of who to fear," I tell May. "I know you're angry about being accused, but war is never a good thing, my prince," she says. I begin to answer, "If that were true, there would be no wars ever. War can be for the greater good, and pretty soon I will decide what's good for Autem."

I see a man rushing out from inside the castle. As he gets closer, I can make him out. It's Edward. "Prince Samuel!" he yells as he is running. "Thank goodness you've made it back in time," he continues.

"What are you talking about?" I say. "Back in time for what?"

"It's your father. You must see him, quick. I fear he hasn't much time left." Without so much as a word, I take off running to my father's quarters, a million thoughts racing through my head. I can't help but think of the last thing I said to him. If he dies before I get there, he'll think I'm happy to see him go. DAMN! Why did I let those words come out of my mouth?

I've always looked up to him, after I saw him in his heyday when he took charge of and ran all of Native's Point. I only got so mad because I had hoped he would see me do the same. I wanted him to see me reclaim Autem's former glory and bring honor to our family name. If I don't make it to him, he'll never know how much he's impacted me.

I finally make it to his room and the sight is enough to bring a tear to my eye. My father barely clinging to life. His nurses in the room with him, trying whatever they can to make him comfortable. "Father . . ." I say with a shaky voice. "Samuel . . . I am glad you've made it back . . ." he answers.

"Father . . . I did not mean what I told you when we last spoke . . . you're going to be king for a long time still yet."

"Well, I believe only one of those things is true . . . Seems there's not a lot of time left for me." He finishes his sentence with a hard cough then starts to continue, "You were such an impressionable child. If only I had been a better example for you. I could see it in you when I ruled, when it clicked in you that everyone else was beneath us. It took a long time for me to realize how untrue that was. When they rebelled and we went to war . . . when we lost and I saw the bodies in the streets; I had seen bodies before, but these where people that I had seen walking about the kingdom. Men and women that had died for my war. A war I had just because I thought the other kingdoms were beneath us. When you're king, I pray you don't make the same mistake I did."

Tears fall from my eyes. I grab his hand and I just sit with him. I sit with him until I can feel his hand go limp, and I lose it. I've never cried like this in my life. I feel angry and sad. Soon, I feel May come behind me and put her hand on my shoulder. "Those bastards made a fool of my father!" I say with anger. "They broke a once great man. He died a shell of his former self." May looks concerned, "What are you going to do?" she asks.

I answer, "Take back what they took from him."

RICHARD

What would my father have done in that situation? He would've helped her out, right? Or, would he have boiled my actions down to prideful ideocracy? Would he have seen a woman that needed help, or would he have seen a way to anger an ally? Oh well, I guess I'll know soon. I've thought about avoiding telling him, but it's better he knows. His guidance on the matter would be much appreciated. After all, I'm still learning the ins and outs of this whole leadership thing. It's best he tells me what I'm doing wrong before people start counting on me.

As we get closer to Gresham, the smell of smoke thickens. As I look out of my cart, a cloud of smoke is above the kingdom. Wooden buildings are on fire, but it's still unclear as to the cause. The closer we get, I start to be able to make out bodies in the street, and my heart sinks in my chest. A group of Gresham troops are outside the front of the town, but I still don't see the attackers. When we pull up to them, before I can speak, one of the troops begins to talk, "Sir, we need help!"

"What happened here? Where is my father?" I say.

"He's in the keep with the king, but we can't get to him. A big group of men came in today wearing no armor, and only had bows on their backs. We didn't think anything of it, we thought they were hunters. They had hidden daggers though. Once inside the walls, they cut through and made their way to the roofs of buildings on the main street. So that means if we try to get by them to get to the keep and help King Timothy, we are going to end up taking fire from their bows."

"Damn it . . . well, we have more men now. How do we go about this?"

"Well, sir, that's up to you. Now that you're here, you're commanding rank."

My father and my cousin are in danger, my city is in danger, and the weight on my shoulders continues to grow heavier. I scan the area. Sure enough, I make out archers on the rooftops. There are enough men here to make it to the castle, but with me leading them, their lives are in my hands. I have got to be smart about this. I lay out my plan. "We can go back-to-back, circular-shaped shields around us, but that's only going to get us so far before the arrows overtake us. Pull our wagons to the side of these buildings, at the edge of the street. With an extra boost from a fellow man, you should be able to climb to the rooftop. If you have a bow, take it to the rooftops. If you have a shield, you're with me down the street. Once we draw their fire, take aim and shoot. We move together until we get to the king."

Deep breaths, my heart is pounding. I get a shield and raise it up in between two other soldiers, up against their shields, making a wall around us. The armored boots we wear will help shots we could take to the feet, but if one man breaks our wall, we are all at risk. Deep breaths . . . now or never. Time to save my family.

I give the signal and we start to move forward. Slowly moving,

keeping formation. THUD! I feel the first arrow hit my shield. THUD THUD THUD! I hear them coming in all around now. Arrow after arrow. "SLOWLY! KEEP MOVING SLOWLY!" I yell. Hearts pounding as the concern for my men grows. Slowly, slowly, OUCH. I feel a thump from an arrow that hit my foot causing me to stumble slightly. A gap forms between my shield and the man's next to me. Before I can fall back in line, one single arrow slips through. "AAHHGG!" I hear from behind me. Shield up, I turn my head to see the damage. An arrow is lodged in the lower back of the soldier across from me. He keeps his shield high, but he's struggling. "If he lowers his shield, we have to cut him lose or we'll be vulnerable," one man says. "Just hold on! Help is coming!" I yell, but I can tell his shield is going to be down soon. With an arrow to the lower back, he's got to be in a lot of pain.

There's so many arrows coming at us, now is the perfect time for

part two of the plan where in our archers will climb onto the rooftops. Sure enough, I hear arrows flying along with yells from the unknown men that were focusing fire on us. With no time to react, they're hopeless to stop our archers from taking them out with ease. It's now clear to make a run for the keep. "Onward for Gresham!" I yell as we run for the doors to save my father!

We bust through the castle doors to find a battle going on inside. No sign of my father or Timothy, so they must be in the throne room. "Join the fight here, I'll search for the king." I direct the men. I move through the room, dodging swords on the way, until I make it to the throne room doors. "I SAID GET THE HELL AWAY FROM ME!" I hear from the other side of the door. I barge though to see Timothy backed up to a corner with two men closing in on him. They're both wearing undistinguishable clothing expect for an armored brace of the right one's arm with a sun engraved in it. Not a perfect match for Autem, looks like he made it himself. It's something to go off, but why would Autem attack us? Alistair definitely seemed to think they had something to do with the burning of his stables. Other than Autems own king, King Timothy is the only other man that stayed behind. Only people at the meeting of the four kingdoms knew he'd be missing a large group of his guard to make him an easy target.

I need to get their attention away from Timothy. "You heard the man." I yell, "Back away!" They turn to face me. With a confused expression, they glace at each other until the one with the brace on says, "What are you looking at me for, get him!" The other one looks back at me and slowly comes forward. He's looking around for a place to strike on his way over. I see his eyes aiming at my arm and then at my legs. He's making a game plan.

Why give him a chance to follow through with it? I lunge at him with my sword. He tries to move out of the way, but I am able to get his shoulder. Not a fatal wound, but I'm sure it's enough disrupt any game plan he had. The shoulder I hit was his sword arm so there is going to be a lot less power in his swings. So, naturally I wait for him to swing. As he swings, I catch his wrist in my hand and slice him in his torso before pushing him aside.

I now set my eyes on the one with the brace. "Looks like it's your turn." I tell him. My temper is high. As he walks over to me, I rush him, swinging hard. He blocks, but before he can swing back, I front kick him in the chest. He stumbles until he trips over a body on the floor. I rush over to him and put my sword through his arm, just above his brace, until my sword hits the wood floor. He lets out a big cry as I start my questioning; "WHY ARE YOU HERE?" I point out the sun on his brace, "DID PRINCE SAMUEL ORDER THIS?"

"Richard!" I hear Timothy yell. I look up at him as he continues,

"Uncle Bruce . . ." he says with a quiver in his voice while pointing over to the other side of the room. I look over to a floor now covered with six bodies. Five of them, the enemy, but the other, my own father, lifeless on the floor. My senses seem to go. It feels like time stopped. I don't know how to feel. I don't know what to do. It feels as if it is me who is dead on the floor. I look back at the man I have pinned down. Almost emotionless, I take my sword out of his arm and drive it in his chest. A desperate attempt to cope with what I am seeing, by sentencing the guilty party. Before I even stand up, emotion floods back into me like a knife in the sole. Deep cutting sadness.

I gather the strength to stand up and walk over to my father. I drop to my knees next to him. I feel a hand on my shoulder as I look over to see Timothy on the ground with me. "It was five versus one. He was able to take three of them out before they got to him . . . I'm so sorry, cousin . . . he told me to stay back, if I just would have done more maybe . . ." tears begin to fall from Timothy's eyes. My young cousin blaming himself for his uncle's death. In reality, if I had left Leonkam on schedule, maybe I could have been here in time to help. "Don't blame yourself." I say, "You were just following orders." I look at my father's armor that I don't feel fit to wear, as it dawns on me that I am now active general.

I look at the grey lion pin he wears that holds the ends of his cape together around his neck. I remember when he had it made when I was a boy. I was so excited about it because it matched up with a story he would tell me as a kid. An old folktale. He told me, "The story of the grey lion goes like this, once there was a pride of lions with beautiful golden fur. All except for the grey lion, who was seen by the others as not as beautiful and, therefore, they treated him like an outcast. All of the other lions boasted, but for all their talk, one day when hunters came, they were cowardly and tried to hide. Together, they could have fought back and won, but they all care only about themselves, so they never even thought to do so. The hunters did not care about hunting the grey lion, because his pelt was not worth much. So, unafraid, the grey lion stood up for the others and scared off the hunters." I would ask, "Why would the grey lion do that when all the others didn't deserve to be saved?" And he would answer, "Did your heavenly Father not save you when he could have left you to perish? When all of us don't deserve to be saved?" I hang on to those words. It gives me a well-needed perspective. My father was a great man. That story shows his humility, something he credited to making him a better leader. It's a story that reminded him as well as taught me that putting others above yourself regardless of what you get in return is what a great leader does. Now, I need to take his words to heart and use them to lead in the best manner that I can. I look at my king next to me. Clearly shaken up and needing reassuring and tell him this, "It's you and I now. We can do this."

ALISTAIR

Prey is always so . . . unexpecting. A thought I have to myself on a ram hunt I am currently embarked on. A ram is a strong animal, stronger when you have to deal with a group of them. But, they have no way to deal with the spear they don't see coming.

So, even the strongest hunter is smarter to hide and wait for the perfect moment. I could draw my weapon, go in there, take the lot of them down, and bring home a feast. A younger me probably would have, but I am older now. If I charge in, take a horn to the knee, and end up with nothing, I bring nothing home to my people, no new mount for my wall.

I stare at a group of rams, young, but decent in size. They may still yet grow. A bigger target to hit with my spear. Passing on them now means greater reward in the future. However, I also grow older. How long can I afford to wait? I know not what tomorrow holds. What if something happens to our crops and our livestock? What if we need the meat from these rams now, rather than later? A good hunter must consider this. A good king can't think of anything other than this.

. . . A good king must see the battlefield as a hunter stalking his prey.

Neal

Imanaged to make a fire after we put some distance between us and the men chasing us. The sun is coming down, and the fire is needed to make sure we don't freeze through the night, even if it could possibly help our attackers spot us. King Adonjay has plenty of enemies so it could have been anyone that organized that attack. I need to keep a close eye out tonight. The king is already asleep by the fire. Best I stay up all night, we are going to have to leave before sunrise.

Time goes by. Hours it feels like, I have no way of knowing how many. My eyes get heavy. Even when I blink, I worry I am not going to be able to open my eyes again. Just sitting here, listening to the peaceful cracking of the fire, is enough to put a man down. Just as I think I am about to fall asleep, I hear something. Leaves being stepped on close by. I slowly grab my sword and raise it. The sound moves closer, and closer.

Out from the trees I see the cause of the sound emerge, a woman dressed in rags. I do not believe my eyes! It's my own mother! I am in shock! I do not know how to react. She is exactly how a remember her, doesn't look as if she's aged a day.

"Is it really you?" I nervously ask.

"I have missed you so much, my son," she answers, as she brushes her red hair back with her hands.

"I can't believe what I'm seeing!" I say.

"Nor can I," she answers, "My own son, the right hand to a man enslaving his people. How can you be an ally to this man, this terrible king?"

"You don't understand! I, myself, am still a slave. What choice do I have?"

"Funny, when I was a slave, I wore rags, and there you sit in some of the finest armor of Native's Point."

I look down at my armor. She's right. Most slaves would dream of wearing something like this. "Not to mention that fine blade you have, and not even ten feet away from you, sleeping, is a man that has caused so much damage to your kind. So much pain, and your blade is the cure. Do what you know you should and inject it into his heart."

" . . . Mother."

"Of course, he is right about one thing. The other kingdoms don't realize how much they need Nalaryia's wealth. If you free the slaves, there is only a matter of time before they want them back. No, no, something will have to be done about the other kings as well . . . ."

"Mother, I have killed in the name of our people before, but it is not that simple. How can you not understand that?"

"HOW CAN YOU SERVE THE MAN THAT KILLED YOUR MOTHER?" she yells.

"He didn't kill you. You are right here in front of me," I say. And softly she answers "No . . . I'm not." And before my eyes like sand in the wind she disappears.

Just then, my eyes shot open. It's daylight out. It must have been a dream, though it felt so real . . . And now I've overslept. "My king, get up!" I yell. "We've stayed here too long, we have to move."

SAMUEL

Today is a bleak day. It all seems to be in slow motion, as the preparations for my father's funeral are being made. The only thing good about today is that I will finally don the crown. Word will get out soon to the other kingdoms, although the official announcement will take place during a meeting that has just been called my Gresham that will take place soon. Although I can only speculate as to why they would feel the need to meet so soon after our last gathering.

I need some air. I step out of the church of which the service will be held. I then start walking in the direction of the nearest tavern to get a drink. Sure, I could call for a nice carriage ride to get there, but why not take my time and really see my kingdom. Just take it all in. I can look out and see the beautiful beach just behind the church. I can look to the great people of this kingdom, working in the stands, selling fruit that is grown nearby.

After some walking, I make it a tavern. I go inside and grab a seat. "Wine," I say. The bartender turns to see me. After a quick look of surprise comes on his face, he says, "Of course, sir, anything for the prince."

"I am not your prince. As of today, I am your king!" I say with a stern voice. "So, I've heard." I hear another voice say from across the room. I look over to see a man with scars on his face. Not yet an old man, but older than I. "Good riddance," he says.

"I could have your head for that kind of disrespect," I respond.

"I know you could, but the thing is, I don't much value it anymore. I have your old man to thank for that." He raises his glass.

"Spit whatever it is that you want to say out. You're losing what little interest I had in this conversation."

"I fought for your father, believed in him. So did my father and brother. They fought and gave their lives for your father's cause. Where the hell did that get us? I proudly wore the sun on my chest. I BELIEVED we were doing what needed to be done, but us normal people we're just caught in the middle of your father's measuring contest . . . ."

" . . . I see." I turn to the bartender. "This man drinks on me tonight. Help him forget he drinks alone, because his family was not up to the task of being Autem quality soldiers." He abruptly stands up like I crossed a line. "Ah, ah, ah." I say, "You've just insulted my father's memory. I could do a lot worse than an eye for an eye. You even get to drink free the rest of the night." He looks at the floor as if to confirm he is going to let it go. I continue "I am . . . aware my father had flaws . . . but what we are doing here . . . we are doing what needs to be done . . . now I would like to drink in peace."

I turn to face my cup, pick it up, and take a drink. Just then, I feel a hand on my shoulder. "What now?" I say aggravated. I look to see May with her hand on my shoulder. Beautiful as always. Showing up when I need her, just like she always does. In a moment when I am low, here she is to bring me back up. "Thought you could use a friend," she says, with a smile. "How about we get some fresh air?" I nod my head, and we leave the pub.

We walk to the beaches. Then, we walk some more along the shoreline. Talking the whole way. Talking is never so easy as it is when I am with her. My oldest friend. Yet, at the same time, it always makes me feel strange. Strange as in, I have been in more than a few sword fights, and I never feel nerves like I do around her.

" . . . Today should be the best day of my life. I have been waiting for the crown from the time I was a little boy . . . Well, I'm sure you remember, pretending to do the ceremony with me when we were young." I say with a laugh at the end. "I just wish he would have put the crown on my head . . . rather than me having to pull it from his dead hands." Her smile sours and she says, "I spent a lot of time with King Wallace . . . toward the end. As proud of you as he was, he felt making you wait was for your own good. You have to believe that all your father wanted was for you to be the best king this kingdom has ever seen."

"You know, a great king needs a queen by his side . . ." I say awaiting her reaction. After a look of discomfort, she begins to speak. "Samuel, I am your adviser, wouldn't being your queen be a conflict of interest?"

"So, advise me from right by my side. I know we have something between us. I have known since we were children, May."

"I know what you mean . . . I do . . . but when we differ as adviser and king, I think I can leave those feelings at the table. However, as husband and wife, you and I are supposed to be one. How could things not be taken more personally?"

"Who's to say we would even disagree on any big issues?"

"Just tell me this, Samuel, what is your goal as king?"

"Well, to give us what we deserve. To put these other kingdoms at our feet, just like it should be."

"That is where we differ. That's not what your father wanted . . . not at the end at least. You still don't see that we don't deserve anything. We're no better than anyone else."

"YOU'RE WRONG. May, the reason I DESERVE to wear the crown is because I know we ARE better. If it were on your head, you would have our people stooped down to the same level as the other kingdoms!"

She looks down at her feet for a second and I can tell I have hurt her feelings. "No, Samuel, I cannot be your queen," she says, just before she turns to walk off the beach.

I just stand there, turning my head away from her, as it feels as if she's walking out of my life as a whole. I turn to the ocean, watching the waves crash into the shore.

Richard

"The other kingdoms have been informed, there is to be an immediate meeting held here, and that we refuse to leave Gresham until the meeting is had. Good idea on that order my king," I say to my cousin. Though, in truth, the idea was mine that I put in his head, but it's good to build his confidence. Making the other kingdoms come here gives us the best chance if one of them is looking for a fight.

Not only that, but it will give me a chance to confront Samuel. I can only hope Alistair will be on my side. It would be nice to count on some backup, and I think he likes Samuel even less than me.

"You think it's Autem? It has to be, right? I saw the sun emblem on that man's brace," Timothy asks me.

"I think so. At the meeting, Price Samuel came off like the kind of guy that thinks everyone is beneath him. Maybe he plans to take full control of Native's Point. We're the closest kingdom to his so it's as good a starting point as any."

"But that would leave them open to getting flanked, as Nalaryia is far west and Leonkam east."

He has a point, if that was Samuel's plan, he didn't think it through well. Not only that, but my father would tell me how King Wallace had gotten to be a man of respect in his old age. As I'm sure he would have had to sign off on any attack, I find it hard to believe he would order a hit on us out of nowhere.

"Does anyone else have any reason to attack us? How did the meeting go?" Timothy asks me. I start to think, maybe Alistair didn't take the news of me stealing from him so well. Then again, the attack had already started before I made it back home, so there's no way Leonkam men could have beat me here if they left after me. "Maybe it was Adonjay." I say, "I kind of messed up his slavery plans. It's not impossible that he was smart enough to frame Autem." This whole thing could be a little more complicated than I thought. My gut still tells me Samuel had something to do with it. Something about that guy I don't trust.

Then I realize that if King Timothy himself is here, the other kings are not going to entertain me as much as last time. I need to make sure my cousin is ready to speak.

So, I do just that. The time passes as we discuss strategy. I find myself enjoying time with Timothy. It has been a while since I have last spent time with the boy, but we are family after all. It's good for him, soon he is going to have to step up and lead our people.

As we talk, a Gresham messenger comes in. "My king, my general." He says. First time I've been called "general." He keeps going, "We have heard back from the other kingdoms. Autem is still dealing with the death of King Wallace, but once Prince Samuel is crowned, they will be heading this way." As if things could get any worse. If Wallace is dead, then that would have left the door open for Samuel to order the attack. It all adds up.

"King Alistair is on his way now. As for King Adonjay, troublingly we have just got news that he has yet to make it back to his home. His kingdom is getting worried. His caravan was last seen riding near the Gresham forest."

Well, that is troubling. Adonjay was the only other suspect. Him going missing so close to Gresham could make us a suspect. Not only that but without him Nalaryia may be a nonfactor in a battle. Leaving us more open to attack. I can only hope more will be revealed soon . . . .

ALISTAIR

My men and I have just stopped to set up camp on the road to Gresham. We could travel straight through, but it has been a . . . busy few days. No harm in letting the men take it easy, especially with most our horses being killed in the fire of our stables, we just have one wagon with us, pulled by two horses. The rest of the men are on foot.

"REST UP, BOYS!" I yell. "Enjoy your selves. Start a fire. We have food and drink in the wagon."

From the corner of my eye, I see Steven walking to join the men. He's been almost silent so far this trip. He's taking his failure against that Gresham soldier hard. Not such a bad thing, feelings such as that are the reason we strive to improve. I have a chance to give him a push in the right direction. I walk up behind him and put my hand on his shoulder. "Come," I say. Without a thought, he does as he's commanded.

We walk together in the forest where we are. Still a ways outside of Gresham. It's a long trip. Longer on foot. We reach a small open space near a large tree, and I figure it's a good as spot as any to have a chat. "Stand across from me and draw your blade," I say. He does, but with a confused look on his face.

"I have been training twice as hard from the time I lost that fight, my king. If what your implying is that I need more practice—" he says, but I cut him off. "No need to be so sensitive. Just thought we'd have a little friendly competition on this nice day." I pull my great-sword off my back. The weight in my hand is more than what I would expect most men could swing. "Show me if any of that extra training is paying off."

Sword in front of him, he begins to circle me. I wait on him to start things off. He comes in with a swing with some muscle behind it, and we clash swords. While held there, I step on his foot and throw my shoulder into the flat of my blade. Pushing into him with enough force to trip him up and knock him down. While he's on the ground, I say, "You're good with a sword, but you have to remember your body is just as good of a weapon in a fight." He stands up. "Again," he says.

We get ready, and this time I come at him. I swing at him hard and when our swords meet, it's enough to knock his sword out of his hand.

"It's not over." I tell him, "Think how can you still win this." I swing at him once more. I swing full force, but am confident he can handle himself. Sure enough, just barely, he is able to roll out of the way. As he is roll-ing out, he reaches to cup my ankle with his hand and pulls my leg out from under me, making me lose my bal-ance and fall to the ground.

I look up, and there is Steven with is hand extended to help me up. I reach to accept it and say, "Fought like a true warrior. To win, your mind must be as sharp as your blade." He smiles and says, "They do say practice makes perfect."

"You know . . ." I say as we walk over to take a break, near a close by tree. "There is no amount of practice that can prepare you for the hardships of being a king. You can't practice being able to sleep at night while your mind thinks about the safety of all your people. You can't practice keeping your sanity, knowing war could be brought to your doorstep any moment."

"Yes, but the honor of being a king . . . to have that many people look up to you . . . it must be well worth it."

"Just remember you said that. You may just get a chance to find out for yourself one day." He looks at me like he's trying to decipher what I just told him. I continue to speak, "I have no wife or child. For the reason of what I just told you. The burden of king is one I wanted on my shoulders alone . . . but I won't live forever. At some point someone will have to take my place . . . I am hopeful that you will show me that man should be you."

His eyes widen. He quickly gets on a knee, bows to me, and extends his sword out to me. "My king, my sword and my life belongs to Leonkam. I won't let you down."

I can't help but smile. It makes me proud that I have brought up good men like him in my army. I have high hopes for the future . . . very high. "Come on, let us go back and enjoy time with the rest of the men," I tell him, reaching my hand out to him. He accepts and we walk together back to camp.

NEAL

How could I have been so foolish as to oversleep? I can hear men hot on our tail as myself and King Adonjay run through the woods. There are so many of them. I don't even know why they're after us. I don't know how I am going to be able to save us . . . I don't know what to do.

"You, slave bastard! Because you couldn't keep your eyes open, I now have to run through the woods. You've humiliated me." I hear King Adonjay say behind me. I can't help but think of what my mother said to me in my dream, as words fall out of that evil man.

"Quiet, my king. We need to move without sound if we have any chance of losing them."

"Quiet?! WHO DO YOU THINK YOU ARE, GREYSON? They're on our tail anyway, and it's your fault. If we make it back to Nalaryia, I will have your head." My heart is racing. My temper is fragile. I am moving fast, but not as fast as I need to, because the king is slow. I turn and face my king, and get in his face. "YOU are too slow so we can't outrun them. YOU will not be quiet so we can't hide from them, and YOU are the whole reason they are after us to begin with. So, if

73

you don't want to die, you have got to listen to me!" I say quietly but sternly. "To think I put you in charge of my army," he answers, with every word he says getting louder. He continues, "I was a fool not to send you off to death with your mother all those years ago." My blood begins to boil.

"There they are!" I hear a voice yell close by. "Oh, no." Adonjay says, "Greyson, you are going to have to kill them." I grab a knife I have strapped to my leg and give it to Adonjay. "Allow me to rectify your mistake . . . I will disappear and make the walk like my mother did. Goodbye, my king." I turn and start to run off into the woods to get away from the men chasing us. Should not be hard, leaving them Adonjay means they got what they came for. I hear Adonjay yell behind me. "Greyson, no! They'll kill me! WHAT DO I DO?!"

"TRY BEING QUIET!" I yell back. Then I disappear into the woods, leaving Adonjay to what's coming to him.

SAMUEL

I have dreamed of this day as long as I could remember. I am just moments away from the crown going on my head . . . it is all I have ever wanted. It's funny . . . well maybe funny isn't the right word, but I always imaged this day a certain way. There I would be, before my father as he put the crown on my head. He would give me a look of approval as if to say everything I had always wanted to hear from him, without saying a word in actuality.

Then, I would look over to my Queen May. She would look especially beautiful on this day. Not that she doesn't every day, without even trying, but this day she would try, and it would show. She would say how she always knew I would make a great king.

Lastly, the other kingdoms would be there, bowing before me. Alistair, throwing roses at my feet. Adonjay, offering me riches and slaves. And little King Timothy, shining my boots.

"King Samuel . . . sure has a nice ring to it." I hear my servant Edward say as he enters my room, breaking the daydream I had let myself get invested in. "The time has come. Are you ready?" he says

"Yes, I am ready." I stand, and put my hand on his shoulder. "Thank you, Edward."

"I know you'll do your father proud . . . You have already made me proud, sir."

I don't need anyone to be proud of me is what I instantly think in my head . . . but that's not what comes out . . . Instead, almost involuntarily, I reach out and hug Edward. He hugs me back and for a moment. It's like he shares my pain with me, as if he saw me loading too much weight on my back and took some and put it on his instead.

After we break, I follow him to the throne room for the ceremony. Soldiers are all that is in attendance. They read the names of all the kings to come before me, and even have a nice little history lesson of everything my father did. Then, they place the crown on my head, and declare me king.

We all head for the main hall to feast. There are soldiers and other advisers there, as well as some higher-end citizens. Everyone is having a good time, but me, it feels. The worst thing is, I can't even place why. They eat and drink just because they have an excuse to eat and drink. Now that I am king, soon they will have a REAL reason to celebrate. Now that I am king, soon my father and May will be proven wrong about me when I put us back on top. Once it is showed just how good life can be when Autem rules all of Native's Point they will see that in reality my goal as king was noble all along.

As I sit, a fire starts inside me, and I decide to stand and tap my glass.

"MEN! You are all aware we have a meeting in Gresham in two days' time. However, I am not a king that would like to wait for them to get their plan together with this emergency meeting they've called. NO, get ready, men! WE RIDE TONIGHT!" I say with anger in my voice. As the cheers of my men echo my enthusiasm.

Then, I walk over to May who I haven't spoken to since she rejected my offer to make her queen. "I won't ask you to come with me, but I still greatly trust your counsel. The choice is yours."

She seems to look like she appreciates that, and says, "And miss the chance to see the new king's opening performance? I will gladly come."

"Good. It's time to show there is new life in Autem."

RICHARD

"Richard, I have something to admit," my cousin, King Timothy, says to me, with a sour look upon him. "I have an uneasy feeling in my bones for this meeting. Truly, I remember little of my father the older I get, but everyone speaks of how great of a man he was. Without Uncle Bruce, I am sure the kingdom would be in shambles by now. He was another highly respected man . . . And you, since having been thrown into to the role of general, you haven't missed a beat. You're so confident . . . it's like you . . . all of you were made for this. Sometimes I feel like an imposter to share the same blood as all of you. Like that part of the Hayward blood that makes being brave as simple as beathing air . . . has skipped over me."

All I can think to myself, having heard that, is that I must have done a better job than I thought, hiding how I truly feel about our current situation. Someone is out for blood, and I still can't be sure of who it is. My father, who is much better a man to handle something like this, I just had to bury. Scared is an understatement for how I feel right now.

"Nothing has skipped you, Timothy. You're just young and that's okay. The amount of pressure you have at your age is something not many can understand, but we have each other. We are family. You can think of me as someone to help carry your burdens."

He looks as if I haven't fully convinced him. Before we have a chance to keep talking, the door busts open. "My king, Autem approaches!" one of our soldiers alerts us. I nod to Timothy to say, "You got this," and we rush to the gates.

Sure enough, Autem wagons are heading for us. Eventually, getting close enough to where I can spot him is Prince Samuel. Now King Samuel, the man I most suspect of ordering the attack that killed my father, leading the charge. Slowing forward, they come right up to us, as the pit in my belly grows. Once again, the same woman is with him from the last meeting, May.

I cannot help but wonder why she, who seems so warm and kind, would want to spend any time with Samuel. We watch as they dismount the wagon and walk up to us. "King Samuel, we did not expect you so soon. We thought you would arrive tomorrow," Timothy says.

"Yes, well, I am sure we're not interrupting. I just couldn't help but want an extra day of that famous Gresham hospitality to celebrate my new role as king. Though, I must say, this place looks as if its seen better days. Whatever happened here?" Samuel responds. As if you don't know what happened, I think to myself. Timothy speaks again, "There's been an attack, and we can't be sure by whom yet. We were hoping this meeting may help us gain prospective."

"I see, how poor for you. Is Bruce off, cleaning the mess?"

My teeth grind. He has the nerve to say my father's name.

"My uncle Bruce died defending us in the attack." Timothy responds with his head hung, "Many were lost in the attack. Gresham is in mourning." Here it is. Now is my chance to gauge Samuel's reaction to this news. I watch closely, but all I see is what seems to be a genuine display of shock. He begins to speak, "I am truly sorry . . . I now know what it's like to lose a father." He says while looking right at me.

Is he trying to play me somehow? How can I trust anything he says? Still, he seems to be sincere.

"Why don't we have our men show you to your room so you may get settled in?" I say, trying not to sound preoccupied with my own thoughts. Them coming early took me off guard, I need time to think. They both nod and they are shown to their rooms.

Hour's pass and they day turns to night. I have already told Timothy to try and get rest for the meeting tomorrow. I have been racking my brain, thinking of all the ways I might be able to stay just one step ahead during this whole ordeal. I have exhausted my mind, but there is no way I can get any sleep. I may as well try and exhaust my body as well. I walk to the training yard, sword in hand, and begin swinging at a training dummy.

The more I swing, the less technical I get. Anger starts to take hold and I picture my enemy in place of the dummy. I should have been there . . . I miss you, Father . . . already I struggle without you.

"Not the most technical sword fighting I've seen but it looks like you can hold your own." I hear from beside me. I turn my head fast and am surprised to see May in the yard with me.

"Yes, well, sometimes it's just about finding a way to blow off steam . . . I take it you're a little preoccupied yourself, to be up and wandering around at this hour."

She gives a slight smile and says, "Preceptive as well, I can see your father raised a capable man." Her expression sours. "I am sorry to hear about what happened, you truly have no idea who is responsible?"

I don't know her near well enough to let her know who I truly suspect, but I feel like I can share a bit of truth with her for some reason. "Yeah, I know who was responsible . . . Me . . . I decided to take a detour after leaving the Leonkam meeting . . . If I had had been there, who knows what would have happened . . . Even if we would have died together, it would be better than being left behind without him."

She takes a second to think about how she's going to respond to my self-pity. She begins to speak. "You wear his armor well." She says taking a glance at what I am wearing. She continues, "God does not make mistakes, General Hayward, and his plan will always prevail . . . You are right where you need to be."

I'll admit, her words made me feel better. "You seem wise, May. I understand why you are an adviser to the king."

She smiles, but puts her head down after doing so, like I have complimented her in the form of bringing up a touchy subject.

"It can be a difficult job sometimes," she says. Ah, so that's what has her up walking around. I know she wouldn't tell me if I asked for details. It would be borderline treason to share her king's personal information, but I do wish to make her feel better, so I just say, "God's plan won't fail. Things will work out." Throwing her own advice back at her. I can tell she's still tense, but again, she gives me a smile to show she appreciates my words. "Try to get some sleep, Lady May." She looks at me with a grin and says, "Oh, I doubt that will happen . . . But I did enjoy this conversion." She turns to walk away and continues, "I look forward to seeing you in action tomorrow, General Hayward," as she walks out of the courtyard.

I look back at my practice dummy, and take one last swing before heading off to try and get rest myself.

ALISTAIR

It's not far off now. Gresham. So close I can see it. As we get closer and closer, the wreckage shows itself. Buildings in burnt ruins, and a feeling of emotional pain looms over. We walk in. As I tie up the horses on our only wagon, I feel the stares from the townspeople. I hear the whispers begin, though I can't make out the words.

I have been here many times before. I know my way around, so I head to where the meetings here normally take place, and take a seat. After a while, I am joined by the new king, Samuel, as he makes his way into the door, and says, "Looks as if Adonjay will not be making it after all, hmm?" I look over to the vacant seat next to me and nod.

Samuel sits right next to me and says, "Ah now, don't be so grim, my friend. It feels like the fun is just about to start." I hold my silence. I can tell the feeling of being a big shot king is front and center in his head. Thankfully, without making us wait longer, our host arrives. The young boy king, and the young man that is general. With Adonjay gone, and King Samuel being a young man himself, this seems to be a young man's game I am in.

Richard throws something on the table. A forearm cuff with a sun symbol to match Autem's.

"This was found on one of the men that attacked us. It seems pretty clear who it belongs to," says Richard, while looking at Samuel. It's a bold move to not even say hello first. In this line of work he'll find throwing blame around too loosely isn't going to help him find out what the source of the problem is. That is if it does get him killed before he has a chance to learn anything.

"Is this some kind of joke?" says Samuel. "You mask your hospitality as a way to trap me here and accuse me? Why say nothing of this last night when I arrived, if you believe me to have killed you father?"

It's a fair point, I speak up. "Because he hoped I would ally with him after seeing evidence that you broke the peace agreement." I say, looking at Richard. I notice a little bit of worry come in his facial expression. I continue, "It's possible that strategy might have worked for him . . . had my men not caught a Gresham soldier stealing from me on the way out of Leonkam, after the last meeting. It seems you who accuses, has broken the peace agreement first."

Richard's eyes widen like prey backed into a corner. Fear fills his eyes.

"Hahahaha, pardon me, I can't help but laugh," says King Samuel. "I come all the way here to meet with you rats, only to be accused of betrayal, when it turns out you, yourself, are guilty of the same crime. You know what this could bring on, child?" Samuel asks. I look to see King Timothy's rage building inside him as he stands up out of his seat. "I AM KING HERE, YOU WOULD DARE CALL ME A RAT IN MY OWN KEEP?!"

"SILENCE, BOY! I AM CLEARLY SPEAKING TO YOUR COUSIN," Samuel responds. "You, King Timothy, are little more than a head to hold the crown. Meanwhile, Bruce's replacement for actually running this SHITHOLE is doing a worse job then I could have imagined." I pan over to Richard who is heated now as well. Samuel keeps going, "What's the matter, Richard? Do you think you should get a break just because poor father died Infront of you?"

"King Godwin, please. No one was hurt in my stealing of that necklace. However, the men that attacked, they were dressed in all black, just like the men that burnt down your stables," Richard says. Now that does make me think, but too bad for him I know exactly what I want to do already. I stand up, "This matters little to me, now. I don't think I can trust any of you. Leonkam is leaving this alliance, from now on we stand alone . . . Samuel, this doesn't have to mean war."

Samuel looks back at me and, after thinking about it, he says, "War is inevitable . . . we've played nice long enough . . . Be ready, Alistair, after I take Gresham, I am coming for you." He walks out and his troops follow. I stand and look at Richard. He must be feeling the pressure. He'll get no sympathy from me though . . . something about him . . . the more I learn about him, he has gone from unassuming to one to keep a close eye on.

Yes, Richard Hayward, if we do meet on the battle-field, I will not take you lightly. I stare at him with daggers as eyes to intend to pierce his soul. Then I walk out, without a word. High time I head home, there are still preparations in order.

NEAL

Hunger sets in as I have been in the woods for a few days. Though, I must say, my time in the forest has gotten easier since leaving Adonjay. That's the other thing, guilt has set in as well. Guilt of leaving a man that was my job to protect to his death. It feels like I am trying to weigh my wrongs. On one hand, I left him to die. On the other hand, what he did to my people in Nalaryia . . . to my mother . . . NO, he had it coming.

I bet he did wrong to the men coming after us too. After all, they have left me be after tracking him down. Alright, I know I am in the right direction to Gresham. Get there, steal a horse, and head on my way to home . . . Funny, it's been a long time since Nalaryia felt like home. What will it even be like for me there now that I have killed my king? Maybe I am looking at this wrong. This could be an even bigger chance for me, a chance to leave this place and start a new life.

With any luck maybe I can run from the monsters of my past . . . but I have never been lucky. First things first, I need a horse. Best I do this quietly, I'm sure by now the word that King Adonjay did not make it back home would have spread. Seeing as I was the last one to see him alive, I am sure there would be plenty of questions.

I keep traveling through the woods, until finally, I come to the road that travels between Gresham and Leonkam. I am close to the area we entered the woods in. It's not as silent as I would have thought this time of day. I hear footsteps and men engaging in conversions. I decide it's best to hide in the tree line and wait for the men I hear coming to stroll by. It does not take long. I see men in armor all with red cloth on them. These are Leonkam troops, and they seem to be on their way back from Gresham. I keep my eyes peeled on them. No horse that I could steal. Figures, after they had their stables burnt down with all the horses inside. Although, I do spot something odd. Alistair Godwin himself is with them. If he's there, the only thing that makes sense is that there was a meeting of the kingdoms. Could be to talk about Adonjay's disappearance. If that's the case, this thing is already a bigger deal than I would like. The kingdoms will be on high alert.

This might prove to be more difficult than I hoped. I need to stay cool. I have broken into hundreds of places before, but here I feel nerves kicking in. It just feels like the end of a long, dark chapter of my life if I am able to pull this off and get far away from here.

After a while, I get to where the kingdom is in sight. An observant glance tells me that sneaking in unnoticed is going to be impossible. There are guards everywhere, on high alert, no doubt. It's almost like they're prepared to be attacked. Going to have to use my wit. With any luck I'll be able to talk my way into getting inside . . . but wait, in my armor I will be way too obvious. Not to mention, I have a reputation as the fastest swordsman in Native's Point. One of these guards are sure to know me and, if that happens, they'll take me to speak with their general, Bruce Hayward.

But what choice do I have? I am a long way from home. Besides, I have always known Bruce to be a good man. Surely, he will hear my side of the story if the reason they are on such high alert is my king's disappearance. With any luck, he'll give me a horse to ride home on. Maybe some food too.

I start to approach the gates. The men lock in on me as soon as I allow myself to become visible to them. When I reach the gate, they finally stop me. "That's far enough," the guard yells to me. "Who are you, and what business do you have here?"

I answer, "I am Neal Greyson of Nalaryia, I wish to speak with your General, Bruce Hayward." A look of shock comes upon his face. He starts to talk "But . . . General Bruce is dead, he fell in the attack a few days ago." Before I can think, another man interrupts, "Stop, you fool! We are at war and you're telling the enemy we are without our general?!"

My goodness what a mess this is already turning out to be. Yet, it just raises the number of questions I have. Seems Gresham was attacked, just like we were. Not only that, but Bruce, a man I respected, and to my knowledge ran this kingdom, is now dead. Also, what's this about a war, and them thinking I am the enemy? That's the first problem I am going to need to fix. The last thing I want, is to be taken into custody here.

"I assure you, I am not your enemy. My king and I were attacked on the road back home after the meeting in Leonkam." I say to them, hoping they will be sympathetic to me.

"Really?" one of the men answers. "The time frames match up. Could have been some planned attack, maybe even the same people that burnt down the stables in Leonkam. I know you're not lying, because right after that meeting is when the news that King Adonjay never made it home came out. You were with him? Where is he now? I am sure King Timothy or General Richard will have questions for him."

General Richard, huh? The man I met in Leonkam. Bruce's son. Makes sense that he would replace him. Although, both him and King Timothy are so young. If we truly are at war, it would be hard to believe they can hold their own at their current age. I start to answer the man's question. "My king unfortunately was not able to get away from our attackers. I fought hard to keep him safe. I would have died for him, but we were surrounded . . . I . . . I was too busy fighting the men in front of us, I didn't see one sneak up behind."

Lying was never a big interest of mine. I tend to take the straightforward approach, but I think that sob story will probably do the trick on these two. I continue,

"Please, I need to speak with King Timothy. I will answer any questions he has, and he may be able to help me get a horse to make the trip home."

"Alright, alright," the second of the two says. "Seems I have no choice. The famous swordsman, Neal Greyson, shows up claiming to have intel that could be useful in the war. I would be a fool to deny you access to the king. Come on, with me."

I follow them through this kingdom, that has clearly seen better days. The mess from the attack here is yet to be put back to the way it was before. Buildings are half burned. They lead me into the keep and right to the throne room. I lay my eyes on the boy, King Timothy, sitting on the throne. And beside him, Richard Hayward, now general. Time to make a good impression. "King Timothy, I appreciate you giving me time to speak with you. I am Neal Greyson, and I come to ask you a favor. As you can see, I am a long way from home, and with no horse, the trip back would be very hard to manage."

Timothy speaks up, "Why is it you find yourself without a horse? No one has heard about you, or King Adonjay, from the time the last meeting took place. Something must have happened for you to be showing up here without him. Is he safe?"

"No, unfortunately my king is dead. We got attacked by men in all black on our trip home. I am the only survivor."

"Men in all black? That's much the same for us. We just had a meeting here to discuss. Sadly, it didn't go well. The conversation was led to war. When we questioned King Samuel, he became enraged. Nalaryia will need someone to lead them in this time. In all likelihood, they could be invaded. All deals of peace are now off the table."

King Samuel? Does that mean Wallace is dead too? Much has happened recently.

"Neal, are you acting commander of Nalaryia?" Richard interjects.

"I am," I say.

"Then, seeing as Adonjay has no son, we will recognize you as king of Nalaryia. With our support along with you being the highest rank in your kingdom, there should be no backlash."

King? Me? I was just here to get a horse and run away from this awful place. Funny how things work out sometimes. Do I even want to be king? I mean, I guess I do, I just never thought about it. This could finally be my chance to end slavery in Nalaryia.

"Of course," Richard continues. "We would need to be able to count on your help in the war."

"You have my word." I say, "Give me a horse and I will put everything in order." From there, I am given a horse and am sent on my way. There is much to do with my newfound title and power. I will bend the crooked kingdom I am from to my will and make it a place worth living.

SAMUEL

I sit on my throne. I sit, thinking of what's to come, all the outcomes that could be. How will this end? I really only see one way. All of Native's Point flying an Autem banner. As I sit, May bursts through the door, "My king, please listen to me, it is not too late. There is still a chance for peace."

"You are wrong, May. Unfortunately." I say, dismissing her before she gets too carried away. I can see it all in her face. Anger, yes, but most of all, worry. "There is no need to fear, have a little faith in your king,I say.

"My king, my role is to advise you, but you refuse to listen. How am I supposed to . . . ?"

"That is plenty, May. You are an adviser, you are NOT queen. I am in charge here. I allow you to give me advice when I ask for it. Other than that, you are just another one of my subjects. Understood?" I ask her. I know that was harsh, and maybe even untrue. She is not just any other citizen . . . not to me.

"I might not be queen . . . but, I thought I was your friend?"

You are, May, I think to myself. Nevertheless, I have to stick to my guns. I have made my choice for the good of Autem. I cannot afford to be undermined with war about to begin.

"Many misunderstood my father, King Wallace. I truly did love him. I looked up to him as a kid. He was my hero, and he deserved respect that he didn't get. Even when he softened, he was seen as a washed up, old dictator. Alistair and the others, they hated him because of how close he was to being the one ruler of all of Native's Point. However, if he had gotten the job done, they would have been scared of him. He'd be second only to the Lord himself . . . He was so much better than all of them . . . Just not all of them together . . . I loved him so much that I will have victory where he did not. I value him much more than peace."

Tears almost make their way out of May's eyes, but not quite. "That was all in the past . . . Your father told you from his OWN mouth he doesn't want war. Why are you trying so hard to prove this to everyone?" says May.

"Because he was WRONG in the end! That version of my father had it ALL WRONG. WHO HE WAS AT THE END DID NOT EVEN WANT HIS OWN SON TO BE KING!" I yell, then softly, I keep going, "Can you believe that? I wasn't good enough for him . . . or you, for that matter . . . The other kingdoms, they don't think I am good enough to be king. But how will they be able to deny me when I take their kingdoms? My father was great, but the choice not to give me the crown was the wrong one. I will make sure everyone knows it . . . This conversation is over, I have to ready the troops. Leave me," I say to her. Right before she turns to walk out, a tear finally falls out of her eye.

It falls all the way to the ground and splashes on the floor. Seems no matter how hard we try we can't stop gravity. This means the weight on my back will someday bring itself to the floor, crushing me between it if I cannot rid myself of it.

I sit a second longer until Edward informs me the men are ready for the trip. All that is left for me to do is send them off. I walk to the courtyard where the men are waiting for me. A whole army full of steel and yellow cloth. "MEN!" I yell, "NOW IS THE TIME. THE TIME TO PROVE THE AUTEM BLOOD RUNS IN YOU. THE FOES WE WILL FACE DO NOT HAVE OUR NUMBERS. THEY DON'T HAVE OUR STRENGTH. THEY DON'T HAVE OUR PRIDE. WE WILL NOT FALL; WE WILL NOT EVEN COME CLOSE TO IT. THIS IS OUR WAR FOR THE TAKING!"

RICHARD

"Thank you for sticking with me in this time, cousin. I know I would not be able to face this war without you," says Timothy. I hate this. He's so young and now war is on his doorstep. I fear greatly for what will happen to him if we lose . . . Will he be set free? captured? or, just killed on the spot?

I can tell he's scared of the same questions. DAMN! He's too young to have an army trying to end his life. This all could have been avoided somehow. I just don't know how. There's so much I don't know, and it infuriates me. Who burnt down those stables? Was it the same people that attacked us and King Adonjay? Come to think of it, Autem is the only kingdom without an attack. It has to be them, right? Or, maybe, a new group entirely, one that wants the four of us trying to kill each other?

I just . . . I just wish my father were here. He also knew what to do, what to say. Now, here I am, trying to lead his army. Men that would have fought harder for him than for me, likely. They respected him, all of them did. As did I. My whole life I just wanted to be my own man. Wanted people to see me as someone other than just Bruce's son. What a fool I am. If I had the chance, if he were here now, I would tell him just how proud I am to be his son. How much of an honor it would be to be like him.

"Timothy, it's time to do what we planned. The battle will be here shortly," I say to Timothy. The plan is for him to stay hidden in the throne room with guards, where he will hopefully be safe. See, we got word that right after King Samuel got home, he sent out his first wave of men to attack us. Seems his plan is for us to already be defeated by the time he gets here, or at the very least, weakened.

Timothy goes ahead, and retreats to the throne room. Meanwhile, I make my walk to the gates of the kingdom, where all our men are waiting for me. Seeing them all lined up, I know this is a good group. I have faith in our men. "MEN!" I yell out to them, "OUR ENEMY IS ALMOST HERE. I NEED ALL OF YOU TO FIGHT WITH ME THIS DAY. THIS WAR CANNOT BE WON WITHOUT ALL OF YOUR COURAGE."

I wait to see reactions, and what I hear is none other than the voice of my training partner, Ridge, "WE ALL LOVED YOUR FATHER. THESE MEN COMING FOR US HURT HIM AND OUR HOME. RICHARD HAYWARD, WE WILL FIGHT FOR YOU. FOR BRUCE AND FOR GRESHAM!" The crowd cheers, and I smile at Ridge to say thank you. Just him saying that makes me feel better about this battle. My large comrade didn't need to speak at all but that's the kind of impact a pure and kind man like the one my father was can have on the world around him. I know we are all fighting for things we hold dear. That is the reason we will give this battle every last bit of strength we can pull out from deep inside our hearts. Then I smile, looking up. "Thank you, Father, for still motivating these men all the way from heaven," I think to myself.

Then, I see it from afar. Autem riding in, quickly. I mount my horse and make one more shout to the men, "HERE THEY COME. FIGHT LIKE YOU ARE FIGHTING FOR THE LORD . . . AND IF TODAY IS OUR DAY TO MEET THE LORD, IT IS A BLESSING NONE THE LESS!" Cheers come from the men again as I ride to the front of the group and toward the Autem men. Racing toward them, heart-wrenching, but somehow feels like the slowest seconds of my whole life.

I just need to be able to fight relaxed, I think to myself. That is when I do my best. In training, when I am relaxed, I am able to move effortlessly, without friction. I don't even have to think, I just do. Here, however, I can feel the anxiety spreading in my body like poison. I can't even breathe without telling myself to. "In, out, in out . . ." I have to think to myself. Come on, Richard, don't freeze up. You are fighting for everything you have EVER known.

Those Autem soldiers in yellow are coming at me with great speed, on horseback. If I had to guess, they have close to as much men as us. Scary to think they still have more to spear on the way. It's no secret Autem has the most manpower of the four kingdoms, but seeing just what that entails, firsthand, is just something else entirely.

Here it comes. My sword is out as I brace for impact. An Autem soldier coming at me with intent to kill. I see the way he is pointing his sword and CHINK. I moved to where it perfectly hits my heavy armor on my shoulder. My sword, however, lands just right and slips under his breastplate into his upper abdomen. Though it didn't cut me, the force of his blade hitting my shoulder was enough to knock me off my horse and onto the ground of the battlefield. I am dead center in the middle of madness. Horses fly pass me at a speed well enough to trample me if one were to hit me. Not to mention, my sword is still in the man I stabbed. I grab my dagger strapped to my leg. I guess it will have to do. Horses are missing me by mere inches, it feels like. The anxiety in me continues to build like water about to boil out of the pot.

One of my own men rides toward me. I can't tell who, with his helmet on, but the fact that he is wearing green is well enough for me. An ally to fight back-to-back with might help my mind manage this madness. As he hurls toward me on horseback with the speed of a freshly released arrow, he reaches out his arm. Extending it to me to welcome me aboard. If I can pull off being able to swing onto the back of his horse moving at that speed, it will be an athletic feat indeed. If I can just get out of the middle a little bit, I can fight my way back in without being surrounded on all sides.

I reach out to take my fellow man's hand so I can attempt to land on the back of his steed. As soon as I touch his fingertips, CRASH! Another horse from the enemy hits him in a head on collision! Just barely hitting me in the process and sending me thrown back to the ground. It mostly missed me, but both the man trying to help me and the enemy lay a few yards away, appearing to be unresponsive.

Now I am in the dirt of this battlefield. From my knees, I make a scan of what's ensuing around me. It is not a pretty sight. Gresham men fighting and dying all around me. What seems like endless Autem solders overwhelming us . . . seeing all these horrible deaths of my comrades causes my mind to overwhelm me. Did I lead my whole army to death in an unwinnable fight in my first battle as general? In a state of emotional agony, I cry out from my knees, "LORD! GIVE ME STRENGTH! PLEASE, GOD! LET ME BE THE BEST I CAN BE IN THIS BATTLE! IF IT BE IN YOUR WILL, LORD, SAVE MY FRIENDS THIS DAY."

I open my eyes, truly just shocked I was not killed during that prayer. I was just doing all that I have ever known to do when I feel overwhelmed. After all, everything is much better in God's hand than in my own.

I two-hand grab my knife and stand to my feet, ready to let the enemy have it. Then, out of nowhere, I feel a rain drop. Then another, then another. The sky starts to pour down, as if God is dropping an entire lake on top of our heads. The dirt turns to mud in a matter of moments.

Just like that, the speeding horses zooming about began to slip and fall about. Riders, all getting off to proceed on foot. With that, the battle is slowed down enough where I feel like I can finally think.

All our forces are relatively close to the edge of the kingdom. An edge set up with archer towers. See, with the speed of horses being a factor, we were forced to ride out and meet them in the middle to prevent them entering the kingdom before the bowmen could take them out. However, now that that factor no longer plays a roll, if we can put some distance between us and them, our archers can take a shot, hopefully lowering their numbers. "FALL BACK!" I yell to my men at the top of my lungs. The ones who hear begin to do just that. Unfortunately, not all of them hear, and some are left to stay swinging swords, unaware that the rest of us are falling back.

As sad as it is, those men that keep fighting are the perfect distraction to Autem to put some distance between us and them. It saddens my heart, but their sacrifice is saving hundreds. As soon as we are far back enough, I signal to the archers with my hand. They are already trained to watch for my signal in a battle like this.

Then, in awe, I watch as the sky above me is filled with arrows, all flying in the direction of the Autem troops. The arrows mixing with the rain make a beautiful storm that strikes down on our enemies, leaving bodies in the mud.

The first wave of arrows does a great deal to disrupt them, as they start to trip over their own fallen men. Still alive, but wounded men are crying out to their healthy fellow soldiers. Then, in the midst of Autem's turmoil, I signal again. For the second time, the sky is filled with arrows. This time, the signal is different. I have signaled to them to keep firing off until they are out of arrows.

Pure chaos takes place on Autem's side. Men dying or crying out in pain. Anyone that makes it past the line of arrows gets cut down by the rest of us in no time at all. It keeps on like this until, finally, they've had enough, and fall back out of range of our arrows.

The amount of men they have left isn't enough to take us. To top it off, they have the look of men with crushed spirits. As they look back at us, all of us Gresham men stand tall. More importantly, we stand together, as one. We watch as Autem moves farther away until we can't see them any longer.

Behind me, cheers erupt! "WE DID IT!" sings out from the mouths of my comrades. I, myself, can't help but smile with relief. "Thank you, Lord . . ." I say softly just loud enough for me and God to hear as part of our ongoing conversation. Then I yell out, "WE WON THE BATTLE, MEN. BUT THEY WILL BE BACK . . . AND WE WILL BE READY TO MEET THEM YET AGAIN!" I shout, raising my sword. "But for now," I say more calmly this time, after the cheering had settled down, "someone go tell the king we can sleep safely tonight."

ALISTAIR

We have made it back home after that eventful meeting. I knew more or less how it was going to go down. Still, things escalated quickly. Both Richard and Samuel lost their fathers recently. It could be they are mad at the world. Needing someone to blame.

Nalaryia will likely be a nonfactor in these upcoming battles now that Adonjay is dead. Still, that means Neal Greyson likely fled. Shame, he truly seems like the only worthy man to meet me in the battlefield. The fastest sword in the land, huh? What does speed mean when you lack strength?

I decide to take a walk outside to take in the view from our city near the mountains. I begin traveling down the stone streets. Unfortunately, these days, the view inside our city has men and women sleeping on the streets. As I walk, I hear, "It's him . . . it's King Godwin!" I hear a rather small man say. Life has clearly been hard on him. His fat has been eaten away leaving behind a skinny rib cage to freeze out in the cold. "What have I done to deserve to life like this, my king?" this man cries to me.

"Is begging what to do for a living? Is there no way you can find to provide money for yourself?" I say to this man, hoping for him to see his time is better spent working.

"My king, I work . . . I cut wood all day to sell to the people here. What I make with it, I can buy some food, but the bulk goes to the tax. That's why I am forced to sleep in a tent."

I look around, seeing that other homeless people have taken an interest in our conversion. They all are looking at me like I owe them something. I do hate that they have to live this way, but it is not my responsibly. No, it is my duty to keep them safe and to protect them. That means we need weapons, and steel costs money, so the tax has to be high. "Would you prefer to live in Nalaryia?" I ask. "There you would be a slave and I would make all of the money you earn. Or would you rather live in Gresham, a place without a natural defense like our mountains or the ocean where you could be attacked at any time? This world we live in is hard sometimes, but I do things the way I do them to keep all of you safe. When this war is over, we will finally be just that."

My words seem to fall on deaf ears as people with hungry bellies have other things on their minds. They just walk away and sit back on the ground.

With hurt in my heart from that encounter, I walk back to my war room. On the way, I stop into my kingdom's kitchen and make an order to the staff, "From now on, soup is made and brought to the homeless outside. Every night, until we are out of food. I eat last, only if there is some left for me." I say, then keep on my way to the war room.

Once I make it, I begin to talk strategies with other military men of mine. I will say, I have missed this, call it a guilty pleasure of mine. What can I say, I have always felt made for battle. Dissecting the perfect way in which to defeat our enemies is the perfect way for me to cool down and take my mind off of what just happened outside.

After long talks about our game plan, everything has been decided. Instead of prolonging this war, we will wait until Autem and Samuel have made their way to Gresham. We will meet the both of them on the battlefield then, after they have already been weakened, and take them both out in one clean swipe.

NEAL

I unmount and tie up my horse outside the keep upon my arrival back to Nalaryia. Nerves begin to flare up feeling like bats playing in my belly. Before I walk up the stone steps and through the wooden doors, I take a glance back at the city that belongs to these grasslands I am in.

Beautiful fields filled with thriving crops. Then, I look back at the magnificent keep made for a king that I am about to enter. All of the beauty in this place was built on the backs of slaves, like me. Us slaves have succeeded in making a beautiful coat to hide the rotting body that lies beneath it.

I have to succeed at becoming king today then I will free the only thing beautiful about this place and build a society that is worth even more than this place's outward appearance.

I enter the keep and am greeted by a view of the great hall with a wooden throne at the end of it. A throne, which sits empty, though the room is not. High-ranking soldiers and wealthy town members fill the hall, alongside angry shouts. From the sounds of it, it seems that in

King Adonjay's absence, panic has begun to take hold of the kingdom. Especially with news of the war beginning.

Upon seeing me, the room goes dead silent. One of the higher-ranking soldiers, a man I know by the name of Grant Cooper—though I don't have much of a relationship with him as I tend to train on my own rather than with the other men—speaks up first saying, "Neal? . . . I can't believe you're alive. We were starting to believe . . . ." Then, with a moment of hesitation, after realizing I'm alone, asks, "Where is King Adonjay?" The look on his face seems like he already knows the answer to his question. Me being here alone all but confirmed what he already suspected. Still, the rest of the room holds on to a little bit of hope. Hope, that I now must take from them with my testimony.

I begin to tell my story. "King Adonjay is not with me. We were intercepted outside of Leonkam by a vast number of men in black clothing. We escaped into the woods, but they kept pursuing us, and soon they found us. I fought to protect him, but they got around behind us. I only made my escape after it was too late to save Adonjay." I take a pause to evaluate facial expressions. Panic in a few of them, worried about the future of the kingdom. I keep going, "I already stopped at Gresham, they provided me with the horse I used to get here. I told them what I have just told you and they decided that as I am the highest-ranking soldier . . . that they would recognize me as the new king . . . I have a letter signed by King Timothy . . . I am here to claim the throne."

Muttering starts in the crowd. I can't make out if it's good or bad, could be either. "YOU CANNOT BE SERIOUS!" a voice yells from the crowd, and a young man maybe thirty years of age steps forward. A tall man, with long dark hair, and dressed with wealth. I recognize him, in fact, I have had an eye out for him for a while now.

His name is Jon Bishop and he is a slave owner here. All of his money he collected from his father as he passed on when Jon was young. This made him an owner just before the cut off for acquiring slaves happened. Yes, he has been a name on my list for a long while. With the guards he can afford, however, he is a difficult man to kill. He starts to talk again, "And why would we let Gresham pick our new king? They have no weight here. They clearly just want you to be king so you will join them in the war."

"Yes, that's true," I say, "but with war coming to our doorstep, even if we do nothing, I would say Gresham is an ally we cannot afford to lose."

"Who's to say we would lose them as an ally?" answers Bishop. "Do you really think they care if you, a slave, becomes king? As long as we offer them help, they will not care in the slightest about who we choose to lead us." Unfortunately, he is likely correct in that assumption. After all, when has anyone ever looked out for my best interest? I need a way to convince them I am best to lead us.

"I am much more than a slave!" I say with all confidence.

"And just what else might that be?" Bishop responds.

"I am the best fighter in the kingdom, even Adonjay admitted that much. He wasn't completely stupid, why else would a man who hated slaves rank me so high?"

"So, in your head, this skill with a sword gives you power?" Bishop asks with a condescending tone. Then he asks, "Don't you know that true power is wealth? Have you not observed our kingdom in the slightest? It is no secret our strength here isn't from our arm; it is from our money! I recommend I be made king! As one of the wealthiest people who live here, surely you all will agree it makes much more sense than giving a slave the throne."

After making his statement, the room goes dead for but a moment, then slowly resuscitates with sounds of soft chatter filling the hall. I need to make my point now. "Let's put this to the test." I say, "The reason I am the best fighter is because I am the best strategist, so let's see just how much your money makes the difference. I suggest trial by combat. I will even give you an unfair advantage to prove I am our best chance at seeing this war to the other side. Find not one, but two of the best swordsmen you know and offer them gold if they, together, can beat me in a fight. If I die, your point is made and I am sure the room will agree you would make a good king . . . But, if I prove you wrong, concede the throne over to me."

Bishop starts to grin, "HA! That overconfidence will get you killed, Greyson. You've got a deal. Be in the courtyard in an hour." He states, then turns to leave the room. I let out a sigh of relief over the fact that he took that offer. I have never been so great with my words.

Thankfully, my sword will decide if I become king. Still, I hope I did not bite off more than I can chew.

From that point, time moves on as I wait in the courtyard to meet my opponents. Soon enough, the hour comes, and Jon Bishop arrives with his two chosen champions. The first of whom has on basic iron armor and carrying a greatsword. This is not the best move when fighting a fast foe, so seeing that ups my confidence. Still, he is a rather large man and is wearing a helmet, so I can't well see his face.

The other of the two men is more my size and I notice he has a spear instead of a sword. Spears can be rather quick, so I may have my work cut out for me if he knows how to use it well.

"GREYSON!" yells Bishop. "This is what you wanted. The battle for the crown starts now!"

So it seems we are not wasting any time. The two men take a stance and start to move in on me. I keep my sword out in front of me on the defensive. Soon, they get in striking distance. So, watching the big one's steps, I wait until he only has one foot planted and then I thrust forward. Aiming my sword for his neck, the most open spot on his armor. Just before I land, he brings his blade up to block, just in time, nonetheless. Though, because he was unbalanced, he begins to stumble backwards, just as I want him to. See, the weight of his sword is too much to move in time to block while stumbling. I move in to take the killing blow, when . . . just as I am lunging, I look to see a spear moving toward my face.

In the last moment I duck to miss it, but it puts me off course from landing the hit I wanted. I back up a little bit to rethink. Gauging this situation is tough as I don't know their exact skill set. I'm going to have to use trial and error, but that is quite the risky game to play. One wrong move could put a spear in my chest.

Alright then, it seems the one with the spear is more than happy to hang back and try and take me out when I move near his friend. Odd, considering the spear is normally used to keep your opponent at a distance, but nevertheless seems to be effective. I've got to play this smart. I grip my sword tight and move in for another move.

I raise my blade up and move in fast toward the big one with the greatsword. He sees me coming and readies himself. Here we go. I pull up for a swing and he flinches to block, but I don't swing at all. I use the small amount of time to roll out right past him. Rushing forward, eyes set on the one with the spear. I gear up to put a finishing blow on him when, "Oof!" I am knocked over to my side by the big man I thought I left behind me.

Seems he was faster than I thought. He was able to adjust and shoulder check me. That hurt a little but nothing too bad. Although, I look up to see a spear heading towards my head. These guys really are in sync. I roll out, just barely, but the spear hits my shoulder. Thankfully, my armor holds up and it bounces off.

"YOU WILL HAVE TO DO BETTER THAN THAT, NEAL." I hear Jon Bishop yell from the sideline. The crowd around us seems to agree, with all the unimpressed looks on their faces.

I think I might have it found out now. You know what they say, the third time's the charm. If they are going to stick to the same plan of defense every time, then I just have to disrupt that plan. I lunge in at the big guy again swinging my sword at his chest. For the third time, he blocks it, but yet again I have him moving backwards. This time, however, I know what to look for. I turn to face the spear coming at me and . . . slice. . . . I strike it just below the blade, on the wooden handle, with enough force to break it off. I hit it with a backhand swing. With my sword in my left hand, my right hand is now free to catch the broken spearhead flying loosely toward me. I grab it out of the air just in time to look up to see the big guy with his sword above his head ready to bring it down on me. With one fast movement I shove that spearhead right in between his chest plate and his helmet, stabbing him in the neck.

As he slides down, I feel all of his weight in my right arm and then . . . Let him fall. I stand tall and face the one who was holding the spear. Now, alone and without a weapon, he drops to his knees. "I give up! You win!" he yells.

"NO! WHAT ARE YOU DOING? I paid you to kill him. GET UP AND FIGHT!" screams a very angry-looking Bishop, but his hired sword just shakes his head and stays down.

"It's over. I won, and I think my point had been made." I say, then I turn to the crowd and say, "People, you have my word. I will fight with all I am to keep this place a safe home if you make me king." Silence overtakes the yard. The glancing of the people starts as they all look to the person to their right or left to see what kind of reaction they have to what they just saw. No one seems sure of what to do.

Then I see someone step forward. The first to make a motion is Grant Cooper, my fellow soldier. He makes a statement, "We are in a time now where we need a strong leader. If war is here and coming to our doorstep, I for one want a warrior king leading us." He says with authority, "Neal has proved before our eyes that he can defy the odds. I motion he be made king."

Then Grant pulls out his sword and takes a knee before me, extending his sword out in his hands as to offer it to me. I smile down on him, then look up to see his sentiment shared by the rest of the crowd. After a few moments of quiet, one by one they start to follow along and bow.

A feeling of relief overtakes my soul. It makes me almost feel like for a moment I am living in a world of make-believe. In my wildest dreams, growing up as a slave, I never believed it possible that I could be king. I wonder what my mother would think if she were able to see me now? If only that dream were also possible. If she were here with my newfound power and title, the first thing I would do is throw her a feast to thank her for being the best mother I could have asked for . . . Damn it! I am supposed to be happy now . . . Why . . . why does it feel like no matter what I gain I will never be able to make up for what I lost?

I look out into the crowd and decide it is time to make my first statement as a new king. "First things first . . . all slaves are now free people. Nonnegotiable."

I hear Jon Bishop behind me. "You must be joking?! I have a right to those people."

I chime in, "I disagree. God himself is the only one with a right to anyone's life."

"Neal, our wealth counts on those slaves." "Well, your wealth should give you the ability to pay a wage for your labor. Now, if you would like to join me, I am heading to your estate first to let your slaves know the good news." As I tell him this, I turn to start my walk towards his estate to do as I said but I hear something behind me. Like the sound of the spear I placed in the large man being pulled out.

Then footsteps coming toward me fast.

"NEAL! WATCH OUT!" I hear Grant's voice yell.

I turn fast to see Jon racing toward me with the spear aiming at what would have been my back. With no time at all to spare I draw my sword out and swing up all in one fluent motion. It just nicks the tip of the spear, but in the untrained hands of Jon, it's enough to free it from his grip tossing it to the ground beside us.

Then, without even so much as thinking about it, having just swung to the left to hit the spear I rotate my hips back to the right as if to be throwing a stone and plunge my sword into Jon Bishop's belly.

"Did you see how fast he was just then?" I hear someone say from the sideline.

"This man must truly be the fastest sword in the land," says another.

All the while, Jon has fallen all the way down to the hilt of my blade. His head almost resting on my shoulder with my blade a few feet through his midsection, he lets out a cough. One filled with blood as I feel the liquid hit my back . . . and, finally, I feel his last breath.

Then nothing . . . he was unarmed. Yes, he tried to kill me . . . but does that mean I really had to kill him? No, he deserved it, didn't he? He had slaves. I have killed lots of slave owners without remorse. Here, though, all these people looking at me. I don't like this feeling of their eyes stuck on me, their new king killing one of his subjects.

I did not have a choice in the matter, I just reacted. Or, did I make my choice long ago when I put myself on the path to having my first reaction is to kill . . . ?

I drop him down. "I wish that did not have to happen," I say to my people. "I will have some men see to it he gets a proper burial . . . Change can be a hard thing to accept. Grant Cooper, please walk with me to the Bishop estate."

Grant nods and comes to join me on my walk. His body language seems a little down. He is a soldier, I am sure he knows I did what had to be done. Still, it was a hard thing to watch. "Cooper, I need updated on what our army has been doing while I was gone . . . Are they ready to move out?"

"Training was as normal as ever. Everything is packed and ready to hit the road. We thought we may have to move out to rescue King Adonjay if we got word on where he may be." "Good, we leave at daybreak tomorrow. Gresham will be counting on us."

As we walk up to the estate, I see around forty men. Very thin, working tending to the animals or weeding the garden. I see women walking around as handmaids around the porch of the manor. I see a little girl, looks to be younger than ten years of age, carrying a bucket of water toward the direction of the cows. She is young enough to have been born after the slavery cutoff. She must be the child of one of the slaves here. So, while she is not a slave in the eyes of the law, this life is the one she is stuck in. As this little girl gets close to me, I wave her over. "You, there, come. Drop your bucket and come here," I say to her.

She makes her way shuffling over to me with a nervous look about her. "What is your name?" I say. She looks up right into my eyes and tells me, "My name is

Datyah." In her high-pitch voice. "My mom gave it to me
. . . it means 'believes in God.' Mother says all we have
to do is believe in God and one day we will have true
freedom. Mother says He loves us."

Just saying that brings a smile to her little thin face.
As it does to mine as well. "Yes, mothers are wise like
that, Datyah," I say with a smile. "Will you help me a
while, Datyah? Help me round up all these slaves on the
property. I have to tell them the time has come. God has
brought them their freedom."

RICHARD

The night looms over us as the sun falls down below the edge of the earth. All of us men sit down by a fire just inside the edge of the kingdom, enjoying a warm meal heated over the flame. Other soldiers are holding their post up farther from the kingdom, on guard to let us know if Autem forces come to make a move during the night.

It would make for a rather nice night if it was not for the sound of our injured men having their wounds treated nearby.

"Richard!" I hear my well-named mountain of a friend, Ridge, approach me. "You did great out there today. Looked like a true general in your father's armor. Hell, with your helmet on, I couldn't even tell the difference."

The second time in one day Ridge's words have struck my heart. Growing up, the thought of trying to fill the shoes of my father was a shadow cast so big I thought I would never hope to escape it. I remember watching him lead drills as a child. Everyone in the yard hanging on every word that dropped out from between his teeth.

Not only that but everyone followed his orders with a smile attached to them.

I remember thinking, or rather feeling, it. These men do not follow him because they have to. No . . . this was respect. A kind of respect I thought myself never able to achieve. In that case, why bother trying. If no one wants to listen to the general's son, I may as well be the lovable goofball slacker that it seems I turned out to be. I suppose hindsight is perfect vison. I wish I never would have shown father that side of me. He did all he could to be a great role model and from his point of view, I couldn't have cared less . . . I hope that some part of him knew how much I admired him. More than anything, I hope he has the ability to look down now and think, "That's my boy!"

I hear a scream from the injured near us. "This is all my fault, Ridge." I tell him and he gives me a confused look. "If I had not taken that necklace in Leonkam, Alistair would have backed us. With him on our side, Samuel would have never had the guts to attack."

I await the backlash I am sure is about to come from the mouth of my friend. He has no idea the reason I took that necklace and, anyway, whether my intentions were good does not matter . . . it was reckless of me.

"General," says Ridge, "I am sure you did what you thought was right at the time . . . You cannot blame yourself. Guys like Alistair and Samuel, you cannot expect them to play nice forever. This was going to happen sooner or later."

I am lucky he is willing to give me the benefit of the doubt. This must be that feeling of mutual respect my father claimed from all who followed him.

"Yeah, well . . . don't get me started on Samuel. That guy is as predictable as an unkept flame."

"I definitely think he is fighting for the wrong reasons, but he is angry and in pain."

"And just how would you know what he is feeling?"

"I would not," answers Ridge with a hard look at me. "If anyone here knows how it feels to lose a father, it is you, general."

Well, this guy seems to be on a roll with the words of wisdom today. He keeps speaking, "It's about my time to go take post on guard duty."

"Go ahead," I say. "And, Ridge, thank you. You've given me a lot to think about."

I watch him make his walk toward the outer line. In the midst of all the stress and worry I am feeling in this time, I cannot help but feel relaxed in knowing the quality of the troops I have fighting by my side. I am truly proud to be a part of this kind of army. One where we would all gladly take an arrow to the chest, without a second thought, if it meant our comrades would make it home to see their family another night.

With this kind of pride in my heart, I am motivated to get up and go ask if there is anything I can do to assist in helping our injured. I make my way over to the sizable makeshift tent they have set up in which to tread our men. I glance back before I walk in to see some of our men wearing smiles on their faces and sharing a laugh by the fire. The smoke that was rising above the trees in the forest behind is now disappearing into the night.

I face back toward the tent, lift the sheet covering the entry, and walk through. The whole room is shaped in a more circular manner with all the hurt men lying on cloths on the ground. Both men and women, volunteers and medics, are moving to meet with each man. Giving them water to drink and to wrap their wounds.

"General Richard Hayward," I hear a soft, feminine voice say my name. I turn to see a very beautiful woman raise up from having just finished giving water to one of the wounded. She stands to greet me. She's tall for a woman, she has dark skin, but her hair appears to be bleached by the sun. "Yes?" I answer with a little look of confusion on my face. She seems to know my name but I, myself, am not sure of hers.

"Don't tell me you have forgotten me," she says to me with a smile. Which only heightens my curiosity. "I am sorry . . . I would say I don't believe we have met, but I guess I would be wrong in that assumption." I answer back with a smile myself.

"It's quite alright, Hayward, you must have fallen off your horse so many times that day you lost your memory." She laughingly explains to me.

"Fallen off my horse? . . . Oh, no!" and like an arrow hitting its target, a memory bursts into my head. I couldn't have been older than nine years of age at the time. My father was taking me to learn to ride a horse down at the stable. This was not my first visit. Learning to ride took me a lot longer than most for whatever reason. The stable keeper was kind enough to help with riding lessons for me.

He was a big fellow, could pick me up and throw me on the back of a horse, no problem. You would think getting upright on the horse would be a sizable chunk of the battle when learning, right? Nope. My old man always insisted I learn to ride on some of the more rambunctious steeds we had available. Which always resulted in me falling off short there after being put on.

As my father would say it, "As long as you are my son, nothing will be handed to you. An easy road is hardly one worth walking." The stable keeper was a kind man and never mocked me for falling off. His daughter, however . . . well, she was snickering on the sideline the whole time . . . along with my father for that matter.

And that brings me back to today, the stable keeper's daughter, a face I can't believe I forgot, standing right in front of me. "Grace . . . ?" I say in disbelief.

"At your service, general." She replies with a grin.

"I can't believe my eyes! How have you been? How is your father?"

"We are both very well. He still tends to the stables."

"And what of you . . . what are you doing here?"

"Well, what does it look like I am doing? I am a medic these days. Actually, your father Bruce is one of the reasons I am here today. In all the time he spent down at the stables laughing with me about your inability to stay on horseback I shared with him my dreams for helping people. With time he got me in touch with the right people in the kingdom and I was able to start my training." She says it with such a confidence about her.

"That is great, Grace! It joys me to see you doing well. However it's me who is at your service . . . I am here to help in any way I can."

She takes a look around thinking about where to put me to work at. "These men are all dealing with pain. The last thing I want is for them to be thirsty as well, but we only have so much water here. We have been bucketing it from a troft outside that filled up in the rain. It would be a big help if you could start carrying buckets over." She says, "Consider me your personal packing mule." I jokingly reply.

She laughs. "Oh, I'm sure you can handle it. You clearly have plenty of muscle . . . you could say you're built for this line of work." She says showing off her beautiful smile again. I reply with a smile of my own as we gaze for a moment. Then I somewhat awkwardly break off by stating, "Well, that water isn't going to bucket itself; I better get started." And head out to fill up my first couple of buckets.

The walk isn't too far. I dip my buckets in and then start to head back, carrying them. If I do too much of this, I'll be sore the next time I need to swing a sword, I think to myself. I bring them all the way back, drop them off, and on repeat I do it a few more times. Enjoying the sounds of the campfire and the sounds of the nearby forest.

But soon the sounds change. A sudden yelling in the distance. "Autem is here!" I hear screams. I run back over to the camp as fast as I can, dropping two full buckets behind me.

"RICHARD!" I hear screaming in a voice I recognize from over where we have men on guard. Please, don't be who I think it is . . . Just then I arrive to see Samuel with a whole army behind him, with Ridge on his knees facing me at the end of Samuel's sword.

SAMUEL

Memories seem to flood my mind these days. Memories of my father when I was young. He was tall, I seem to forget that sometimes, as toward the end he rarely stood. Sun-kissed skin tone the same as everyone else in Autem. A very sharp and commanding face before age changed it.

I remember following him around, attached to his coattail when he was around. Of course, he was normally too busy, and I would have to stay back and be watched by Edward. Still, I learned a lot watching the man he was. This one time he let me sit in with him and his advisers. They were discussing raising the tax for the Autem people. This was a short while after the war had ended.

Our financial officers know a cut of the tax from the people pays for their own lifestyles. They were more concerned with their own pockets than anything else. My father, however, opposed this point of view stating, "Would I raise the tax of the people when I wasn't able to raise the amount of land we hold for them?" Referring to his failure to claim the other three kingdoms for Autem. The room we were in is the same as the one May and the other advisers use to meet with me now. Not large, but on the second story of the castle, with a window overlooking the town below. Father said looking out that window reminded him of his true duty as king.

The financial officers did not much care for my father's response to their proposal. One of them went as far to get angry with him. "Just why should we let that affect our income?! We deserve more!" the man yelled to my father, the great King Wallace Gregory . . . I could not believe the disrespect. Father kept his calm about him. See, a man with his power did not have to throw a fuss to get his way. He just looked at the man who just yelled at him, who was dressed in fine expensive clothing, and said, "For all the wealth you wear on your frame, under that is your own body . . . your life itself. Which is a tax you owe to me . . . you would be wise not to forget that."

And just like that the man backed down. Father did not need money to rule . . . he did not even need people to like him, let alone agree with him . . . they feared him. Then and there, I learned that is more than enough.

Now, here I stand today, commanding that same fear as my father once did. I already had the rest of the Gresham guards out here on watch taken care of but this big one stood out as a perfect one to make an example of. This fellow must be the biggest man in Gresham's army but kneed down at the end of my sword, I have gained the ability to make him look small compared to myself.

Across the field I see him. Richard Hayward. No mistaking him now with the green cape he wears draped over his armor. The one Bruce used to don in all our previous meetings. At the end of the day, maybe, we really are just two boys playing dress up in our father's clothes . . . Not that it matters, at some point every son must pay for the debts their fathers' owe. I plan to claim that debt . . . all of Native's Point is owed to Autem . . . is owed to me.

"RICHARD!" I yell across the field between us, hoping the distance isn't too great for him to not hear me.

"You see what I've brought with me, no doubt!" I keep going, referring to the size of my army behind me. "For every archer you have, I have two. Same for every sword." I say, as I grab the prisoner in front of me by the back of his shirt and press the tip of my blade right up against the middle of his back. Not yet piercing him deep. Just enough to draw first blood.

"Samuel, please! You don't have to kill him!" yells Richard back to me. Seems he can hear me loud and clear.

"That's the thing, Richard! You cannot stop me. You cannot stop any of what's about to come to you." I say, then I look at the defenseless man before me and I push my sword through his back.

"NOOOO!" I hear the cries and shouting from the Gresham side of the field. And the man on my sword takes his last breath. Then my own belly turns upside down, it falls inside me. I feel as if I am about to throw up. Killing an unarmed man must have pulled strings in my heart I did not believe it would have.

I had to do it. I had to make this point . . . Richard . . . he needed to see this. "Richard. You have accused me of murder. Now look where it landed you. This is what you so desperately want me to be . . . I did not kill Bruce . . . but tomorrow, I WILL kill you. You can't stop it any more than you could stop me from killing your friend here. Tonight, you live only so you can spend the night in fear of what tomorrow holds." I say, glaring daggers at Richard.

We hold eye contact and, surprisingly, he doesn't break it off. He doesn't say anything, but he holds eye contact with me. How is he able to do that, look into the eyes he must now fear, without looking away in cowardly fashion?

After a moment, as much as I hate to, I break off our stare. I cannot just stand out here all night. I start to walk back to where my men have begun to set up camp for the night.

I catch one of my men on the walk and give him orders, "Be on guard tonight, just in case, but I am sure they won't make a move when they are outnumbered this heavily. They're going to want to buy all the time they can before they have to fight us."

I walk into my tent that has just been put up. I take a seat on a bed that has been prepared for me. A little cot with straw and feathers packed from home to give me a comfortable night's sleep.

I start to unstrap my armor. New armor I had made to carry out my first battle as king. Something to really grab the attention of those who oppose me, so that everyone who sees knows right off the bat that I am king. Steel . . . shiny, fit perfect to my frame with a bright yellow sun painted on the chest, showing I am proud of my kingdom. Attached, a cape with yellow edges but black overtaking the rest of the area. Black to show I might bring death with me when I come. Even the helmet I will don tomorrow has a mane of yellow going down the center of it.

Everything about it was set to make a statement. Yet, as I sit now, looking at my armor I just finished taking off on the floor, I start to question myself. How could it be that Richard was able to match my eyes? Does he have something up his sleeve for the battle ahead that makes him think he can beat me? No! There is just no way. He has to know, most likely, his death is coming tomorrow. Why then . . . why is he not afraid? Damn it, why?

I am overthinking again. I have noticed about myself, I tend to fixate on things. Things that drive me crazy, but soon that will be a thing of the past for me . . . If I can just take Native's Point, everything will be perfect . . . everything will finally make sense.

I lay on my back looking up at the ceiling of the tent as I hear my entryway get moved open. I sit up fast to see who has come in, worried it could be a guard to tell me that Gresham has made a move. To my surprise, I look up to see May Duchsen herself standing in my tent.

The look she wears on her face is calm and stoic. "I thought you stayed back in Autem?" I say to her. "No, I . . . I needed to come see this through to the end."

To the end? She must be meaning the end of the war. "May, it is unsafe for you to be here." I tell her trying to show I still care about her, something our last conversation may have made her question. She turns her head to look me right in my eyes and says, "I remember looking in those eyes the first time . . . we were kids. Seeing the way you played with all the other kids. Demanding to be a leader. Ruling the play yard with joy in your heart. Truly, I don't think I would be the person I am today without you inspiring me. You always made a point to claim what you wanted. There was a time I thought I would be your queen one day Samuel."

I sit back looking at her with no words to say. Wishing I could find anything to say that would mean something to her, but I just sit back at a loss. All the while, she keeps staring right into my eyes.

"But the joy in your way of ruling is gone now . . . I have feared for a while that the kid I used to know is gone now . . . But after watching what you just did, I know for sure that he is. Samuel, I promise you I will always have love in my heart for you."

"May, I love you . . . I do, you must see that." I say to her in desperation.

"Samuel, loving means I cannot enable you. I have to leave this life and you behind. Because that boy inside you is never coming to the surface again . . . I see that now." She says that but she keeps looking into my eyes . . . but I cannot look back into hers. I drop my eyes to look at my feet.

After I do that, I start to hear her steps walking away from me. Before she is out of the tent I say, "May, please, don't go . . . I just need to do this, then everything will make sense," with a shaky voice and tears in my eyes. But her footsteps don't stop and soon she walks all the way out of my life, and I can no longer hear her.

Tears leave my face and hit the floor by my feet.

"I can do this, May . . . I promise."

MAY

My heart feels as though it could beat right out of my chest. I hate that it's come this this. Even if part of me is just proud of myself for finding the nerve to tell him how I really feel and not just live my life going along with the madness he plans to bring to this land.

People always did used to joke about how little May is always quiet until you make her angry and I guess I just proved them right once again.

But an even bigger part of me is heartbroken that I have seemed to truly have lost my best friend. Outside now, in the night, I look at the moon that is covering us and let out a prayer standing out here with no direction. Speaking to my Lord, just as the weight of the world feels like it is about to flatten me, always seems to help me find the strength to put my burdens back up and carry them a little farther.

A practice that I have had to use regularly as of late with how stress packed life in Autem has become. Here in Gresham, however, under the blanket of night with the trees of the forest nearby playing music in the wind, peace feels like it is with me. As I ask the Lord to take these anxious feelings from me. For some reason, under all the hurt today has brought on my soul, this feeling of peace I have now makes me feel like I am right where I need to be.

Before I end my prayer, I pray for Samuel. I pray that somehow peace will find him, and his stress will be put to rest. He still feels that no one understands him, but I think I have begun to. For the most part, he rambles on about bringing honor to his father, only sometimes letting it slip that he actually wants to bring honor to himself and prove that his father was wrong for not giving him the crown. Two contradicting philosophies that sound more like nonsense when he mixes them up, seeming like Samuel himself is not even sure what he's fighting for.

But under it all, as his friend, I feel he is just a boy, heartbroken. Trying to make the world make sense after he lost a loved one. Even if Samuel cannot put it into words, Richard and Alistair aren't the ones he is mad with. They are little more than an outlet to pour his rage into. No, Samuel is mad at life itself. More so the fact that no matter how hard we may struggle, there is just no way we could ever hope to control every aspect of our lives. He believes that if he can control Native's Point, he can take control of his own life, making the narrative fit whatever he thinks will finally bring him happiness. A level of control that is a right reserved only for God. Funny, the person that might just understand Samuel the most right now is the one who he has chosen to rage a war against.

Richard Hayward is another young man born to a high family in his kingdom who is now seeking vengeance for the death of his own father. I bet if those two could put down the swords, not raise their voices, maybe even set aside the political talk for a while, they would learn they are a lot alike. The kind of pressure to live up to a well-respected father can be a hard mountain to climb. Harder if you try to climb it alone.

I wouldn't even rule out the chance that Samuel could make peace with Alistair in another world. Alistair is respected, just as Wallace was, and I know he can relate to Samuel's pride for the kingdom you come from. As well as the want to have everything under his control. I've watched Alistair for a long while now and I don't think there is any mistaking the reason he doesn't have a family of his own. Under the scary act that he puts on, he has a mountain he is constantly struggling to climb, one he will never see the top of. He has a deep fear of loss. I can tell because of the amount of work he puts into holding on to what he has.

Alistair loves his kingdom with all he has, but he always looks like he hasn't slept every time I see him. He has a kind of attachment that even the thought of somehow being unattached keeps him up at night. There's a reason he is the only king left from the last war. Having a family on top of that is something I'm sure his stressed heart just couldn't take.

But that's enough dreaming about what could have been. I have a goal to accomplish in the here and now.

The goal being to sneak over to the Gresham side of the field and have a conversation with Richard Hayward. I walk out a good amount away from the Autem camp before I try and keep my head low and walk through the field. My biggest worry is that if I am seen by Gresham, they might shoot off arrows first and ask questions later. I take my steps slowly and carefully.

It is not a wildly long distance to cover, I would guess less than a hundred yards. Under the cover of night, I think I just might get there. I start to close in on it when I hear a thud. I notice an arrow has placed itself just a few feet in front of my feet. Heart pounding, I look around to see where it came from when slice, another arrow hits me, just grazing my left shoulder, opening a wound on it.

Panic kicks is as I realize how easily that could have hit my chest. I don't believe my athletic ability is good enough to outrun arrows, and even if I could, it still would not get me to a meet with Richard like I want. I decide it best to stand and throw up my arms, all the while yelling "DON'T SHOOT! DON'T SHOOT!" hoping the sound of my female voice will alert them that I am not a soldier and I mean no harm to them.

As I stand there with uncertainty, knowing that now with me standing I am an easy target to be taken out, I hold my breath just waiting for a well-placed arrow to end me . . . but it never comes. Instead, I am treated to two Gresham men coming out to meet me and march me back to the Gresham camp.

Upon arriving at Gresham's camp, I am treated to a somber group. Understandably so, they just saw one of their allies die in front of them. Glares of the Gresham people pierce me and leave a pain worse than that of the arrow that hit me. They make me feel like I am a monster. Maybe I am for not leaving Autem right after Samuel sent the first wave of soldiers to Gresham. I thought I was doing everything I could do.

I had hoped I could stop Samuel if I was near to him . . . make him see reason . . . but I failed. Maybe I am guilty for all this by association. A perfect accomplice just because I choose the wrong words in some of my talks with Samuel. Maybe it even started earlier than that with a choice I might have made when we were young that I could not have possibly seen the long-lasting repercussions of. Something as simple as an idea that got planted in his head . . . but I guess I will never know if I could have done anything to stop this in our past. Today is the present, it's happening, and I have to deal with that.

They force through the entryway of a tent they have set up. And I start to see a sight I wish I had not; the product of this war. Wounded soldiers all over the tent, some in worse shape than others. They sit me down in a chair and walk out of the tent but stay right near the doorway, close enough that I can see parts of them when the wind blows the sheet covering the entry.

Soon, someone comes to greet me. A woman holding bandages and wraps. She gives me a look of discontent like she isn't sure if she should spit at me or not. "Well, let's see that shoulder then," she says taking a look at my wound. "You . . . you're going to treat my wound?!" I say in shock. She looks up at me and says, "Against my better judgment, yes . . . Wouldn't want it getting infected."

I guess I should not be so surprised that even during a war Gresham hospitality is on full display. "My name is May . . . ."

"I know who you are . . . everyone does." She cuts me off.

"I see. Hopefully you heard all good things." I say trying to lighten the mood. She doesn't crack a smile and just keeps working on my cut. After a bit of silence, she says, "I'm Grace."

"Well, nice to meet you, Grace . . . and thank you for helping me." I reply. Again, no response from her.

From outside the tent, I can hear a conversation starting. "She is right inside, general. Good thing we grabbed her. She could be a very useful bargaining chip for us." Richard must have got word that I am here. The sheet from the entryway gets pushed aside and Richard walks in.

I did not get a good look at him before; he was too far away. He is dirty. His very impressive armor stained with mud. His green cape that drapes over his chest and down his back has the bottom a nasty brown now. It makes sense, I had heard that rain and mud played a role in the first battle.

"May? What are you doing here? You could have been shot down!" somewhat angrily asks Richard. I know the man very little but for what I do know this response fits him. He puts others first and cares what happens to people.

"I came to see you. I think we need to talk." I say to him. He acts like he is thinking about what to say next. He looks at me, then he looks at Grace. "Well . . . I suppose if Grace has finished wrapping up your cut . . . we can go talk privately."

"You cannot be serious?" Grace interrupts "She's from Autem. What if they sent her here to kill you?"

Richard looks over to me and responds with his witty charm, "As capable as I am sure Lady May is, I think I will be able to manage." Grace moves closer to Richard. Very close. "Just please be careful," she says. Then she delivers me a dirty look before exiting the tent. She really seemed worried about him. Do I pose that much of a threat? . . . Or, is there something more going on between them?

"Shall we?" says Richard. I accept and he leads me outside and over by a nice, quiet area, campfire still visible in the background. "How's your shoulder?" Richard asks "I think I will live." I tell him with a smile.

"Good, then what is it you have to tell me?" he asks. Where do I start? I feel it's important he know Samuel's mental state is low so he can decide what he wants to do. My instincts as an adviser want to tell him run. Fall back and group up with Nalaryia and hope that them, combined, can stop Samuel. Unfortunately, truth be told, I am not sure anything I have to tell him will prove useful at all to him. I just could not stand to be on the wrong side anymore.

"I deserted Samuel and Autem." I say, "What I have to tell you is . . . just that . . . I am so very sorry . . . I am sorry for your friend that was killed, that was the last straw for me. I left right after . . . and I am sorry for not leaving earlier. Not doing so might have caused you to think I support this madness."

"May, slow down. This isn't your fault," I take a breath. Seems I was rambling. I slow it down and say, "King Wallace would not have wanted this. Samuel is confused. He thinks this war is to restore his father's honor. All this has little to do with your accusations at the meeting."

"About those accusations . . . May, do you know if Samuel ordered the attack that killed my father?"

"He wasn't king at that point and all the men were loyal to King Wallace. It is extremely unlikely that he could have ordered that attack without Wallace finding out . . . ."

He looks down at his feet. "You know the last thing my friend said to me before he was killed was that me and Samuel might have more in common than I think. I, also, made hasty decisions after my father passed . . . Maybe all this could have been avoided."

"Samuel is letting his pain consume him. He has reached a point now . . . staring into his eyes I can tell he is lost. Like his old self is falling into an abyss. A place where all his hope has died. A place I don't think he can be pulled back up from." I look into Richard's eyes as he listens to me. "But you have felt loss as well . . . I don't see that in your eyes." I tell him.

"That's humanity you're describing, May. We all will have a day of sadness, heartbreak even . . . but to experience that kind of sadness, there had to have been a type of love that far outweighed what came before . . . and for that I am grateful. We all have to live life. Why hate it when you have the power to do all you can to enjoy it?" He looks back into my eyes. "And in those times life gets too hard . . . don't do it alone." He tells me.

Genuine and caring, words I am now sure describe Richard Hayward. He doesn't monologue to get me to believe him, he says what he says because he believes in his words. It's the same reason he sometimes goes against the grain because he believes in his cause. It's an admirable trait even if it does get him in hot water from time to time.

As much as Samuel Gregory and Richard Hayward have lived similar lives they have landed on two different conclusions. Only one of them will make it to the other side of this war. I look up at the moon yet again as it looms over us. I have made my choice, come this time tomorrow, Gresham will either come out victorious . . . or, I will fall along with it . . . No going back now.

ALISTAIR

Obsession. That is what training has become in my life. That is the thought in my head as I stand in a training yard picking up a large stone and throwing it over my shoulder . . . only to pick it up and throw it again. Obsession, that's what drives me to pick up the stone and throw it again after it has hit the ground each time. Even though after every throw it gets harder and harder to pick up again.

Obsession is the reason I am going to win this war. Because my obsession allows me to be out here training while my opponents rest. It is the very reason I haven't lost a battle up to this point. Any man who dared stand to face Alistair Godwin is a man that is no longer alive or a man that I granted mercy to.

Fighting took to me like bees to honey. I was always able to count on that too. When anxiety in me was heavy, I always remembered that I am a fighter, and I can beat the odds stacked against me.

My mother was a fighter before me. She was killed in battle when I was young. With a father who died of sickness before I was born, I was left alone to run a kingdom at thirteen years old. That's when my obsession started.

So that I would never die to leave my family alone without me. I always wondered if my mother had the same obsession of being the strongest as I have. If then I would have been able to grow up with a mother, if she wouldn't have died that day . . . and I wouldn't be alone.

I remind myself I am not alone. That Leonkam is the only family I ever needed. I love my kingdom, that's why I train so hard every single day. Because a man that cannot fight is a man who doesn't love his family.

The choices I have made, I made them all for a purpose. To keep Leonkam safe. So much time has passed for us to get to this point today. War. The choices I made were a contributing factor in bringing us to battle. Of course, the other kingdoms had choices to make along the way as well, but when I look back . . . there is just truly no way to know if the choices I made . . . the things I did . . . were the right ones.

But that's a fool's game to play. Like trying to guess where lightning will strike. We can't change the past, but we can make an impact on the future. At least that's what I believe. I wouldn't care to fight in this war at all if I didn't think that. The future I see is one of peace, but it has become clear to me that violence is the only way to achieve that.

All this time spent collecting high taxes, working hard to make strong weapons. Adding to our army. Playing nice FOR YEARS as we grow stronger. Preparing for a time such as this . . . Yes, I planned for the future, and I believe it's all about to pay off without a doubt.

At this point, sweat has washed over me like a bath. I seemed to have got so lost in thought I lost count of how long I have been out here training. As I see Steven approaching me, I don't know if it's the fact that I know tomorrow's battle has the chance to be my last, or just my old age making me soft. But I have grown to see Steven as a son to me. He grows in leadership ability every day. I am very proud of the soldier he has become.

"My king, I have got everything ready. We can ride whenever you give the order." He says to me. "I am ready now . . . let's not keep them waiting," I respond to him with a smile. The future begins now.

SAMUEL

Today is a day I felt was coming for a long time. A day brought here now as a direct effect of my actions. A day I thought that I was ready for. Standing here now, watching the sun peek its top up over the Gresham forest with the words of May replaying in my head from the night before . . . I am just not sure how I feel.

I didn't get not even a second of sleep. Rather, I just lay there in bed, tossing and turning about in my otherwise empty tent. A feeling of being completely alone is a feeling I fought all night. Knowing that my last friend in the world that isn't my friend because of my Gregory last name has now walked out of my life.

And what's worse, is no horse left out of our camp last night and there is no way she started walking back to Autem. No, she must have walked right over into the arms of Richard Hayward and Gresham's forces. She has picked her side now. The question that has been on my mind all night is when we take Gresham today, will I be able to kill her?

She's the enemy now, right? When the time comes, that's what I should do, but I am not sure I am going to have what it takes to do it. I know for sure that there was a time I valued her life enough that I would have never even considered being the one to end it, and that fact weighs on me. It makes me really wonder if what she told me about me losing the me I used to be holds true. Does she have a point, or was she just trying to get in my head?

Still, now is not at all the time to dwell on that. Daylight means one thing at this point. It means that the battle for Native's Point is starting. Today, the Hayward family story ends so that mine can take the limelight. As I look out over the field that will soon be the location of all this bloodshed, I notice just how nice a day it is for this battle. Not a cloud in the sky.

No chance for rain means that we can speed our horses right across the field and Gresham will be forced to meet us in the middle. If they don't, we will break through, and the fighting will be done inside the town. Meeting us in the middle will buy them time but, before the day is down, our forces will outnumber theirs and we will take the keep.

Richard Hayward should have just bowed before me when he had the chance. If there is one thing I will enjoy about today, it will be seeing his body dead in the mud.

My troops are all rounded up on horseback, ready to move in. Time to give them their parting words, as I will be sitting back and watching the action from here. "MEN OF AUTEM!" I yell getting their attention. "Today is the day we write our names in the history books! Years from now when they ask how it was that Autem conquered all of Native's Point, we will tell them that it all started with this battle today under King Samuel's command!"

And with that, cheers erupt. Hundreds of men cheering at my every word. I will be the reason we win today. Soon, hundreds will turn to thousands telling tales of my greatness. It all starts right now as all of our ears are greeted to a noise of a horn from Gresham's side of the field. Meaning it's time to fight. Gresham horses start to ride toward us, and I give the order for my men to go meet them. I walk over, in my armor fit for a king, to a well-protected part of camp where I can still see the fighting and take a seat. The steeds meet in the middle of the field with great force and the bloodshed starts.

I could go out there and fight myself; I am all too sure I would enjoy killing those peasants, even. However, what good is it to be king if you have to do your own dirty work. Still, I am quite well trained with a sword. If for whatever reason this battle drags on, I might go in and have some fun.

My father often didn't ride out to battle when the first war was happening. He was just well enough staying in Autem and sending our men off without him. Just another way I am willing to do what he is not. To think, the last remaining man that apposed my father is Alistair. King Adonjay is likely to be dead after he has been missing for so long. General Bruce is dead and gone. Soon, Alistair will follow them to the ground, because as soon as we finish here, I am riding east, right to his doorstep.

Although, truth be told, if it was me versus him, one on one . . . Well, let's just say he would be on a short list of people I would not feel confident about beating. His size alone would make for a hard day. It's implied he can break through iron when he swings his greatsword with his full might. Best to just let my army defeat his army. Those are odds that sound much better to me.

I continue my gaze out on to the battlefield and sure as ever soldiers draped in yellow start to overtake the ones in green. An easy victory, just as I knew it would be. Won't be long now.

"Sir, do you see that?! Coming in from the west!" one of my subordinates catches my attention. I turn my head to the west and squint my eyes trying to make sense of what exactly it is riding toward us. The closer they get, the more I can make it out. Nalaryia soldiers. What are they doing here?! With Adonjay gone I planned for them to be a nonissue. Led by a speeding horseback rider, they cash into the fight and lend aid to Gresham. With them together, the size of the army we have to fight is closer to our size, but not quite as many troops still yet.

This definitely will make things a lot harder.

"I bet that's Neal Greyson leading them. The fastest sword in the land!" my subordinate says.

"SHUT UP!" I snap back, putting him in his place. I wish to hear no gloating of Neal Greyson's great fighting ability. He is just a man. Clearly a dumb man at that if he thought striking a deal with Gresham could save him.

"No, no, no, no." I start muttering. "I did not come all this way to lose here. In fact, it is disrespectful to think that Nalaryia would even try to save Gresham from my hand . . . nothing can save them now. I am going in to kill Richard Hayward and Neal Greyson myself." I say as I lower my helmet down on my head as it seems the time has come to fight my battles head-on. I then go to mount my horse and ride into battle.

NEAL

Not since the days of Moses has there been a slave come into power like I have today. Still seems unreal to me. In fact, on the way here one of my men called me "King Greyson" and I did not even realize he was speaking to me.

I thought my life was meant to tell a different story, most likely a tragedy. Now my story has a chance to be a noble one. The story of Neal Greyson will be the story of the man who ended slavery in Native's Point and made sure it never returned.

That's the reason I fight today. King Samuel is a loose cannon who has shown he cares little about my most passionate political issue. If he wins this war and is the one king of Native's Point, there is no guarantee he won't put back the old policy of Nalaryia. Not to mention, my title as king would be stripped from me. No, that cannot happen. Me being on a throne is the ONLY way to keep the slaves free. I made a promise to my people that I intend to keep.

Riding through the battle that rages on is pure chaos. Bodies are falling left and right as I frantically search for General Hayward. Him staying alive is crucial to the efforts of Gresham. Without a leader, an army fights without directions like a chicken that has already lost its head. If that were to happen, my own chances of winning this war would be far decreased. Nalaryia's army isn't near large enough to hang Autem's. I just hope I am not too late, and Richard is still alive somewhere in this sea of violence.

He is likely near the front line. He seems like the kind of man to lead his troops from ahead. I ride forward weaving though the madness. Up ahead, I see an Autem solder eyeing me as I ride towards him. He places himself right in my path with his greatsword in hand. I have little time to change direction and, in this environment, a horse is hard to keep under control.

I must commend him for his bravery, as this Autem soldier holds on to his position as a 1,600-hundred-pound animal comes hurling toward him like he's content to play a game of chicken with it. Closer and closer I get to him until the horse gets spooked, pumping its breaks and rearing up on its back legs until it is almost vertical to avoid the crash. However, this sudden change in angle throws me right off the back of my animal. I land flat on my back as it knocks the wind out of me. It makes me struggle for breath like I may never catch it again. I have felt the feeling of losing air before, but I know it puts me at a big disadvantage for the next couple moments until I can recover.

Seems I will have no time for that, however, as I open my eyes to see the same soldier that caused me to get bucked off standing over me. His greatsword raised over head ready to bring it down on me. As he throws it down with intent to kill, I narrowly roll to my right just out of his target area. I am able to roll all the way up to a knee before he lifts his sword again. For the second time, he raises it over his head to bring it down on me. While true, the axe swing can generate a lot of force, it very much leaves you open to attacks from a faster swordsman, and I just so happen to be the fastest of them all.

As fast as I can, I grab my knife strapped to my calf and plunge it right through the top of his right foot. He yells in agony as his sword comes down toward me. I sidestep the blow as I raise to my feet all in one clean motion. Then, I front kick his hands which are in perfect placement for me to do so as they are still low to the ground from swinging his sword. This knocks his sword out of his hand. My knife is still in his foot and my sword on my back. Without time to draw it, it looks like it's time for a fistfight.

He comes at me swinging with a wide haymaker. This guy just seems to love to go for the power blows. This will be his last one, however. He will not have another chance to learn his lesson. I duck it and while underneath I am face level with his gut, which I take the time to throw a hard left jab and a straight right into.

He hunches over in pain from just having his wind taken. This gives me the perfect opening to grab his neck in a guillotine choke. With the back of his neck up tight against my armpit and my forearm wrapped around his throat, I quickly drop to my back pulling him on top of me and wrap my legs around his waist so he can't escape. Then, turning my wrist so the bony part of it that connects to my thumb is the main thing making contact with his throat, I squeeze. He struggles at first. It's not until after close to sixty seconds I feel him go limp.

I roll his unconscious body off me and resume my search for Hayward. I keep powering forward near the front line. Looking for his green cape, as the last time I was here he was the only one wearing one. At this point I pull my sword off my back and have it at the ready.

Along the way, I have a few opportunities to slash a few enemies, which I gladly take. Finally, I catch a glimpse of it. A green cape fighting hard ahead. Good thing I got here when I did, he is on his way to being overrun.

Sure, the cape looks flashy, but it definitely does not help when the enemy is targeting you. He is doing his best to stay up, but he is backpedaling hard as three Autem men are on him. He is doing the right thing keeping them in front of him so as not to be stabbed in the back, but at the moment all he can hope to do is block attack after attack with the Autem men not giving him any chance to strike back.

I approach from the left of the encounter, and before they even realize I am there, I place my blade through the side of the Autem soldier closest to me. He drops as I pull my blade out. The other two turn to face me, giving Richard the perfect opportunity to finally strike back. He takes his chance and strikes the soldier closest to him down with a clean swipe. Just like that, the tides of the fight has shifted from three-on-one in favor of Autem to two-on-one in our favor. On the battlefield, things can change in the blink of an eye.

Still, the last remaining foe is armed with a shield and sword. This is likely the best weapon choice for going against two foes at once. This could be a challenge for us, provided this Autem soldier knows how to use his tools well. Richard and I shuffle toward each other, all the while keeping our blades pointed at our enemy. Until we come shoulder to shoulder facing our opponent.

With no time to exchange greetings, Richard gives me a look. One as if to be telling me "I'll go first" to which I reply with a nod. I welcome this chance to see what he can do in combat. It's something about this young general I know little about.

He steps forward twirling his sword, a rather confident aura about him. As they get in range of each other, Richard rears back with both hands gripping his hilt and takes a swing from right to left. The Autem soldier wisely extends his shield out to block. Forcibly, the sword and shield are about to connect . . . but no, wait. Hayward tilts his sword up right before the hit lands, taking away its reach and not letting it make contact with the shield.

Instead, he keeps his momentum from the swing, and follows through into a spin, releasing the hilt with his right hand to make the turn faster. After flying around in a full circle around him, Richard's blade has picked up speed and slams right against the edge of the shield, knocking out of the Autem soldier's hand.

When he first faked a big strike, the Autem soldier extended to block. Had the first swing been real, it would have worked with the blade landing in the middle of the shield, but after the fake he did not have time to pull his shield back close to him. While extended, the heavy shield takes a stronger grip to hold on to, meaning that when Richard spun around to catch the right to the edge it was enough to pull it out of the soldier's hand. Smart move.

I am impressed. I have always felt battle is not an exact step-by-step routine. To put yourself in the highest heights of being a warrior, you need creativity. A good battle intellect.

I do my part. With the foe off guard, I move in for the finishing blow. With a second to catch our breath, Richard says, "Good thing you guys came when you did, things were starting to get hairy out here." We are still outnumbered here but he keeps a good attitude on him. "Yeah, well, better late than never, right?" I say back to him. "Exactly, I never once lost faith that you would show up and keep your word, King Greyson." He responds to me.

His words show gratitude. It means something, the fact that he will acknowledge me as a king. I will go a long way to help others acknowledge me. After we win this battle, that is.

"We are outnumbered still yet," I tell him. "If we want to end this with the most lives saved, we have to find King Samuel and kill him. As fast as we can."

"That's not going to be easy, there is just no way he is out here fighting like we are. Not with the manpower he has. He will be deep behind enemy lines. Impossible to get to."

"I am not sure you're right about that. Look!" I say as I point over to an Autem soldier farther up on the battlefield. Dressed in armor fit for a king. "I cannot tell for sure with the helmet on, but my guess is Samuel felt he had something to prove and got out here for himself already."

"That's him, alright," Richard responds. "That's what he was wearing yesterday . . . When he took the life from my friend." Richard says with a quiver in his voice. The conflict between him and Samuel seems to have hit a boiling point a while ago now. From the outside looking in, the hate between them has extended to new levels.

Still, Richard is going to have his work cut out for him. True, I saw that he is no rookie in a fight just a moment ago, but from where I am now I also have a good look at Samuel. He, himself, is engaged in fighting with Gresham troops. He holds a surprising amount of skill I did not expect out of him. He is very good with his blade. Fast and well disciplined. As a king's son, I am sure he had top-of-the-line teachers his whole childhood.

Watching him strike down Gresham troops, I cannot help but feel Richard will need my help to win. I do, however, expect with the both of us, side by side, Samuel won't stand a chance.

"We need to make our way over there. Side by side, we will have to watch each other's backs and fight our way there." I say to Richard. He looks over at the ground we are going to have to cover to get where we need to be and responds, "Yes, I agree." He thought it over a little bit it seems but, ultimately, he seems fine to defer to my judgment. As I am the older warrior.

Hopefully his trust is rightfully placed in me, I do not wish to let him down. Back-to-back, sword in hands, we start to move our way over to where Samuel is fighting. However, in a crowded battle, a few feet can feel like miles. Every step, a new opposing swordsman in our path. Still, Richard and I seem to fight well together. Slicing down foes with relative ease.

True, he is not on my level yet, but I would say he has the potential to far surpass me as he gains age and experience. Moving closer and closer I take glances over to Samuel fighting when I can afford to. It doesn't take long before he spots us. I don't want to miss our chance; I was hoping he would not notice us. If he hightails it and runs, we won't be able to end this war.

Instead of running, however, he does something I wouldn't have guessed him to do. He points his sword at us. "HAYWARD!" I hear him yell vaguely over all the noise around us. As Samuel starts on a death march toward us, I think to myself that I always assumed he was all talk. That when push came to shove, he would not do his own dirty work. I guess I was wrong. And happy to be wrong, as King Samuel's overconfidence is about to get him cut down, ending this war.

"Richard, now is our chance to end this; don't rush in. If we fight him together, we are sure to win." I say to my ally.

"Right!" he answers with a nod.

Here we go, this is it. "WAIT. LOOK! WHO'S THAT RIDING IN?" Richard exclaims. I look to the west to see what looks like hundreds of riders on horseback coming into the battle. Crashing in from the back side of the fighting and attacking the Autem men. No, wait, not just the Autem men, but us and Gresham too! The red cloth on their armor gives it away, it's Leonkam for sure!

But how?! Alistair claimed most of his horses were burned in his stable fire. This doesn't make any sense. He is KILLING everyone. Was this all some sick lie to round us up in one spot so he could destroy all of us? That bastard!

Looks like they are riding right towards us. A horse carrying the large frame of Alistair Godwin stops right up in front of us. Richard, Samuel, and I all watch as he dismounts and says with a stern voice "Good, you're all here."

ALISTAIR

The time has arrived, here on bloodstained land. It cannot be helped. I am here for a reason. To end this war, my way. "Alistair, I don't understand. You said all of your horses were burned in your stable fire. We saw your stables burnt down when we were in Leonkam. You said you were attacked!" I hear the confused voice of young Richard Hayward.

"Even used it as a reason to end the peace agreement between us, if memory serves," King Samuel Gregory throws his words into the conversation.

"Well," I begin to speak, "seeing as today will be all of your last day, I suppose I owe you the truth." I watch as all of them have their eyes glued to me, waiting anxiously to hear what I have to say. "In the last few weeks, we have all been attacked by unknown foes dressed in black. King Adonjay was attacked on the road, Gresham was attacked here, at their home, and my stables were burnt down. All of us but Autem took a hit . . . and now I can tell you that this was by design. I ordered the attacks, even burnt down my own stables to avoid suspicion, of course, not before moving my horses to safety.

This, mixed with the reckless attitude of Samuel, was more than enough to put him on everyone's suspect list."

"You framed me? You're psychotic!" Samuel yells at me.

"I did, but you can't say I was not true to character with you. With little convincing at all, you marched all the way here to start a war and kill hundreds. Which is why I felt the need to do what I did in the first place."

"Just what does that mean?"

"It means you and King Timothy are young and reckless and not fit to be kings! It means that with me getting older every day, the only true way to ensure Leonkam's safety is take you out now, while I still can! Taking your kingdoms now will be the true way to keep peace long after I'm gone . . . And I knew the best chance I had to do that was to have you fight each other to a weakened state before I joined the battle."

No, this was not a choice that came easy. I thought long and hard about it but, in the end, I cannot just keep a peace agreement with people I don't trust. Leaving my people . . . my family to the mercy of children and insecure men who act on a whim.

"Alistair, please call off your men! It's not too late! No one else has to die!" Richard pleads with me.

"Are you mad? Did you not just hear him?" Samuel interrupts "No, no, someone definitely has to die! As a matter of fact, this changes little for me now. I still wish to kill the whole crazy lot of you! Alistair, all you have done with your plan is shorten your own life! After I am done here, I will make sure Leonkam burns to the ground!" Samuel raises his sword, ready to fight.

"SAMUEL, YOU'RE JUST PLAYING RIGHT INTO WHAT HE WANTS," Richard yells.

"ENOUGH!" Samuel yells back at him, "I have had enough of you, or any of you for that matter, thinking you know better than me. It is you PEOPLE THAT ARE DRIVING ME MAD! . . . Whose fault it is does not matter at all anymore . . . you all have to die . . . it's the only way." A very brief moment of silence fills the air, waiting to hear what Samuel will say next.

The way he is carrying himself . . . if he hadn't snapped already, this conversation is sure to have done the trick. He has reached a boiling point and just went over the edge.

He begins to have a soft chuckle that turns into a full-on laugh. "None of this matters," Samuel says, like he just had a realization. "It's kind of funny when you think about it."

"I do not find the humor in it at all, boy." I answer to Samuel.

"The battle raging on around us . . . people dying for these causes that the four of us happen to feel so strongly about to risk our lives. And none of it matters because the real war is right here between the four of us. The winner of our fight will win the war and all the other lives lost will be meaningless. The only thing that matters now is becoming the one king over Native's Point," Samuel says. "You're wrong, Samuel. All of our men have a role to play in this war! I won't have you disrespect their sacrifice!" Richard yells at him.

Once again, Samuel chuckles, "There you go again, Hayward, always sticking up for the little guy . . . I would just love to kill you first!"

Samuel takes up his sword and sprints over across to Richard, ready to take his head off. Richard braces, Samuel gets there and puts a lot of weight behind his first swing. Aimed right at Richard's head. Clink! blades collide, but it's not Richard's. At the last second, Neal jumps just in front of Richard blocking Samuel's blade with his own.

The speed at which he was able to move was impressive. I had never got to see it with my own eyes, but I suppose he truly is the fastest sword in the land. "Richard, stay alive!" Neal says to Richard as he and King Samuel engage in a battle.

This leaves Richard and I alone to have a battle of our own. I ready my greatsword and say, "I will take no pleasure in killing you. I am just doing what I feel is right." My words are the truth, if I had felt this could have been avoided, I would not have done what I did. However, this was bound to happen. No matter what.

He readies his sword as well. "Alright then, I guess there is no avoiding it."

"The other three of us are kings," I say to him, "and you are the lone man without a crown. You are also the youngest and least experienced, and you are forced up against me, the oldest and most experienced. I do hope you put on a good showing, let's see what you've got, Hayward."

"I'm not worried. Seems to me like you've aged out of your prime." He responds. Insults are what I would expect out of a boy like him.

He runs in to strike first. I block and push into my sword, shoving back and causing him to stumble. "You're pretty strong," I tell him. "Bet you're used to being the stronger opponent in your fights. Tell me, have you game-planned for someone like me that you could not hope to out strengthen?" I say, imposing my strength on him.

"Yeah, well where there's a will, there's a way," he says, running right back in again. However, his witty remarks will not help him in this fight. This time I swing before he gets there, with so much power that when I hit his sword it blows it out of his hand. Then I follow up with a hard front kick to his gut, sending him flying back. "UGH!" he lets out a sound of pain.

"You will need more will than that to beat me! Come on, did your father teach you so little?" I ask him. He stands up, clearly in pain, but runs in again anyway. Unarmed, so I suppose this is where he dies. I jab my sword at him when he comes in, but he ducks it and, while below me, he throws dirt up in my face, making me lose him from my sight for a moment. He rolls out as I take a swing of my best guess of where he is. I miss.

On his way out, he picks his sword back up and points at me. "Good!" I say. Releasing this fight could be more competitive than I thought. "Now, show me something!"

SAMUEL

I keep on the offensive, sending blow after blow his way. My goal in mind is to keep him on his back foot, moving away from me. Swinging at him in a way that he will be too busy blocking to swing back.

The last thing I want is for Neal Greyson to be on the offensive, trying to take me out. True, I have heard tells of Neal's skill with a sword, but I never thought I would get to fight him myself. Years from now, this story will be the one that is told. The famous Neal Greyson's defeat at the hands of King Samuel, the conqueror.

Sooner or later, so long as my wind stamina holds up, one of these attacks will land. While he is doing a good job blocking, it also takes him effort to block my strikes. This means I can turn this into a game, who has better lungs.

"You've been trained well. Must be hard to find good competition." Neal speaks to me during the heat of our battle.

"It would be harder for you, I would imagine. In Autem, my average training partners would be much higher quality than you could find anywhere else, I am sure of that," I respond.

"And what makes you so sure? It is no secret that you see yourself far above us 'other people,' but when you really look at the facts, what tangible evidence do you have for being so great?" He says back to me.

What a silly question. I make a statement back to him, "After this fight, I will hold your decapitated head in my hands. Is that tangible enough for you, slave!" He jumps back, putting more than a sword's length between me and him. Damn, now he might have a chance to swing back, got to do something, quick.

"That's right, I know all about your humble beginnings!" I tell him. "What? You think Adonjay didn't brag about his little pet?" I need to get under his skin. "Do not worry, little slave boy, soon you will be reunited with your mother." I say with a smirk.

Maybe that crossed the line, but I am far past worrying about that kind of thing now. "That's not going to work. I have been in more battles than you can think of. I know how to keep my composure," Neal says to me. "However, if I were to start talking about your father, I bet I could get more of a reaction out of you."

Damn, he's right. Just the mention of father stirs up anger in me. He had better not say anything out of line or he will come to regret it.

While thinking of this, he lunges at me with extreme speed. Come on. I have to stay on my toes. Chink! Our swords hit, but a thought comes to mind. Here is where I may have a chance, but it's going to be risky. I wait for his follow-up attack, a jab from his blade.

Instead of blocking it, I take a big risk and sidestep it, making him miss, and move past me just a bit. I have got to be one of the only people to ever move fast enough to make Neal Greyson miss. I can win this! I grab his extended arm with one hand and, without time to point my blade down, I punch him across his face with my sword hand.

But I keep my grip tight to his wrist making him unable to swing at me. I step my foot between his legs and run an inside trip by placing it just behind his foot and pushing my body into his, causing him to trip and fall to his back. I keep his sword arm isolated and cover him in a half mount. In this position, my body is covering his leg that has his knife strapped to it, making sure he will not be able to grab it and use it on me.

With my sword hand free, I do my best to rise it up in a position to stab him. He is proving to be strong, however, and holding my balance good enough to finish him off is starting to look difficult. As I go to raise up my sword, he takes his free hand and pushes against my hip making just enough space for him to bring up his foot and place it up to that same hip. Then, he forcefully kicks me off him, before quickly rising to his feet.

Back at square one, just much more tired this time. I can see him breathing hard as well . . . He is wearing out, that's for sure. The exchange took a lot out of the both of us. I need to end this soon.

For a fighter, there is no worse fear than becoming too exhausted to defend yourself. So, this is it! Do or die!

I charge him and with power I throw an overhead ax swing with my blade. He lifts his sword to block me. The force of the collision brings him to his knee while our blades are still mashed together. I keep on pushing, hoping to get him to yield, as things are not looking good for him.

Just then, he jams his blade to the right, causing his hilt to catch my blade, throwing me off balance a little past him. All in one clean motion, he grabs his knife from his leg, stands, and backhand swings it. Stabbing it deep into the center of my back.

My eyes widen. I let out a gasp for air to try and catch my fleeing breath. Then I fall face first on the ground. I hear Neal run off knowing our battle is now over.

AH! IT HURTS! I take what little strength I can get and roll onto my back and look up into the sky. I suppose it's true what they say . . . your life really does flash before your eyes when you're in your final moments. I see glimpses of father . . . and ones of May. Both out of my life now are the only two people I ever loved, all because I was trying to prove to myself I was worthy of their love. With the life leaving my body, I stare into the clouds above. I think about something I always wish I could have shown them but was never able to put into words in my time here . . . Father, May . . . I just wish you could have seen my true heart.

RICHARD

" I am about to show Alistair all I've got," I think to myself as I charge in, swinging my sword. Only to be met with a block and a swing in return that is strong enough to send me stumbling backward.

"You are boring me, Hayward!" Alistair says, running in to try and end my life. I dive to the left, just barely avoiding the hit.

"You still don't see what you've done! All these people and you don't even care!" I yell at him, referring to the soldiers dying on the battlefield in the war raging around us.

"I care enough to do what had to be done to protect my people!" he yells back.

"At the expense of my people . . . of my father . . . YOU TOOK HIM FROM ME."

"Bruce was supposed to be at the meeting that day. If you hadn't come in his place, he would still be alive . . . Although, I am sure your cousin, the king, would have been killed if you were the one protecting him. I have no regrets for what I did. If your father was alive now, you would actually have a chance to win this war."

"SHUT UP!" I yell, getting frustrated the longer I think about this situation. "Bruce was a great man. He must have died ashamed that his only child was not able to measure up." He says trying to get under my skin.

It's working, I am boiling. Unfortunately, a small part of me wonders if he is right. Was my father disappointed? Are there things I could have done more to prove myself to him when he was here? One thing's for sure, that's the kind of question I never want to ask myself again. So, from this day on, I will never wonder if I could have done more. I will always give it my all. Every single thing I have, in everything I do. I will remember the words that are written and work as if I am working for the Lord Himself in all things, and make sure my father is smiling down on me from above.

Time for a new approach. This time I run in and slide, trying to swing at his legs and take them out. However, he jumps over my sword and turns to grab me by my cape which he uses to throw me.

I land on my stomach and lift my head to hear the earth shaking. Footsteps running toward me. Alistair gets to me before I can stand and kicks me in the face causing me to flip to my back. He then drops his knee onto my chest hard taking my air.

I try to reach up to punch him, but he catches my hand; and, using both of his hands, he breaks my wrist as I try to struggle. "OWW!" I let out a yell.

I continue to try and kick and fight my way out, but it seems impossible with all of his weight on me.

"Take comfort in knowing you are going to die for a reason," he says to me as he grabs his sword.

"Alistair, don't! There can still be peace." I plead with him.

"Your cries will not be heard by me. We are far past peace . . . For what it's worth, I am sorry it had to be this way." He says to me with what seems to be a truly genuine tone of voice. He raises his sword up about to send it down through my chest.

Come on, Richard, keep fighting. I can't give up now. As the blade starts to come down, I give all of my remaining will power to fight. If this is how it ends for me, I trust the Lord's plan, but while I still breathe, I will cling to the life He gave me!

Neal

"Not going to make it!" I think to myself as I a run at full speed to where Alistair and Richard are fighting, having just left Samuel lying face down with no time to spare. I sincerely hope he went quickly. I take no joy in anyone's suffering. Especially a boy that young. Sure, he played a big part in all of this pain, and I don't regret killing him. He had to be stopped for the safety of my people. Still, young emotions can blind all of our logic.

I move as fast as my legs will carry me as I try and make the run without being interrupted by the battle going on all around us. I can see their battle is not going well for Richard. As I look to see Alistair on top of him with his knee in his chest.

Not very surprising, I hate to say it. Richard is a strong fighter but the strength and size alone of Alistair puts him on a whole other level. Other than if Richard had a stroke of luck, this fight was bound to end this way.

In fact, in a one-on-one with Alistair, I am not sure I, myself, would even have a chance. That's why I chose to fight Samuel first. I had to hope I could take him out fast and Richard and I could fight Alistair together. I knew

I could take out Samuel faster than Richard could but, still, the fight took longer than I thought.

And now Richard might be killed before I can help him with his opponent. I watch as Alistair raises his sword to end Richard's life. I am not going to make it in time, I am still too far away . . . However, I am in throwing distance. In a desperate attempt, I take my sword and chuck it with all my strength, really putting my shoulder in it.

The blade flies through the air making its way all the way to hit Alistair right in the hand that is gripped on to the hilt of his sword. Lobing off his pinky and ring finger on his left hand, causing him to drop his sword and grunt in pain.

I keep running toward them until I am within striking distance. I throw a knee to the face of the unsuspecting Alistair, knocking him of Richard. Alistair quickly hops to his feet while I help Richard up.

"I think my wrist is broken . . . I can't move my hand," Richard says to me. I look at it and it is easy to tell it's broken as his hand just seems to be hanging off his arm. "Well, you'll just have to use your other hand," I tell him.

We stand side by side across from Alistair staring us down with blood dripping from his hand. All of us are unarmed at this point. It will be a hand-to-hand fight to the death to end this war.

"Richard, I need you to have my back, attack only when you see a good opening. Find a sword if he gives you a chance," I say, as I put my hands up and go in to start this fight.

He is much bigger than me so, as we engage, I throw jabs and front kicks trying to keep him from getting too close. "I was hoping I would get the chance to fight you, Greyson. Too bad you're less of a threat without your blade," Alistair says to me.

I respond by throwing another kick, but he grabs it and tucks my leg under his arm pulling me into him. Not good. With his free arm he punches me, showing me just how strong he is and knocking me straight to the ground.

He stands over me about to pounce, but right before he does, Richard catches him off guard and hits him in his ribs. I take my chance and scramble to my feet and try to double leg take down Alistair. Although, it feels like hitting a brick wall. I am not able to force him to the ground. Instead, he grabs me and throws me off him. When he turns to face me, however, he forgets about Richard, who jumps on his back and throws his arm around Alistair's neck to begin to choke him. I watch it unfold as Alistair tries hard to get out, but with as deep as the choke is, he isn't going anywhere.

As his air is taken from him, he drops to his knees. Gargling for breath. He is about to die. With the time I have, I grab my sword just in case.

"Alistair, I am sorry it had to be this way." Richard pleads to him as he takes his life. "I promise you, Alistair, I will make sure the people of Leonkam are safe, you have my word . . ." He says as Alistair's arms go limp, and he stops fighting. The great King Godwin is no more. The moment takes hold as I look at him. He was truly one of the great kings this land has seen in his prime. However, doing what he did boarders on unforgivable. In the same turn, however, if he did not start this mess I would not have become king and gained the ability to free my people. Mixed feelings flood my brain.

Richard promised him that he would keep his people safe, even after everything he did. I do wonder if that is true as I stand behind him with my sword, as he lets Alistair's body go.

Is he truly trustworthy? How can he promise to keep peace with people from other lands and keep them safe when he doesn't know what the future holds?

Who is to say that when his kingdom needs money, he won't come to Nalaryia for slave labor? After all, he is now in charge of an army bigger than mine and there is no more peace agreement.

No, I can't take that chance. Right now, I have the opportunity to take him out and become the one king of Native's Point. Then I can truly ensure that slavery will never return to this land.

I raise my sword up behind him and, as I do, I notice the setting sun cast my shadow over him letting him see the action I am attempting. "Neal . . . ?" he says, "we don't have to . . . become the monsters they tried to make of us." Richard says in a soft voice. Almost like he is agreeing not to resist. Giving me the choice . . . leaving his life in my hands . . . trusting me . . . .

It's a simple sentence, but if I am forced to think on it. This whole war was caused by monstrous acts. Things that I have tried to save my people from. And now, with this one action, it seems I have come close to being just another pig in the mud, committing horrible acts to innocent people. Not unlike the ones committed on my slave brother and sisters.

I drop my sword in disbelief that I almost took Richard's life. "Richard, I . . . Forgive me," I say.

He looks at me with a soft smile and says, "It's okay . . . It's over now." And the sun sets on a hard day.

RICHARD

After the deaths of Alistair and Samuel, the Autem and Leonkam armies backed off and the war was over. Now, a week later, Timothy and I are entering Nalaryia to have a meeting with the four kingdoms to sign a new peace agreement.

It will be us, King Greyson and the new King Steven of Leonkam. He confessed to knowing about Alistair's plans and is under surveillance, but his fellow soldiers vouched that he can be a good leader and well, letting them elect him to be king is a good way to show trust to the new allies.

Our last member is the new Queen May of Autem. A person who, I admit, I am excited to see. She is proving to lead Autem in a new direction.

"Richard, I hope this meeting goes better than the last," Timothy jokingly says to me.

"As long as we don't start another war, it will," I laughingly say back. Timothy is growing into a better king each day and I am truly hopeful that he will surpass us all and be a great king.

Once we arrive, I see the welcome sight of my new friend Neal Greyson who tries to greet me with a handshake, to which I show him my still broken wrist, and offer him my other hand to shake. He laughs and says, "Glad to see you're healing up."

"Well, it would not be broken in the first place if you had thrown that sword a little sooner," I tell him. We laugh together standing here outside but it seems he has something on his mind as he looks over to a group of younglings training in the yard with wooden swords. "That little girl over there. Swinging her stick with all her might. Her name is Datyah, her mom was a slave I just freed . . . this morning she told me she was going to train hard every day so when she gets big she can be just like me. All of this is so new to me . . . being king and all that comes with it. Truth be told, I don't think it would be wise for anyone to look up to me." He says like he is just speaking his thoughts out loud.

I respond, "Neal, look where you started my friend! You stayed true to yourself your whole life and it brought you from a slave to a king. Who wouldn't look up to you? So you've made mistakes along the way? The thing about life is it keeps going and every sunrise is a chance to be a better role model. I for one have no doubt that's exactly what you will be for the young of your kingdom." He smiles at me and puts his hand on my shoulder. "We really can make a change in Native's Point, my friend," he says back to me, letting me know my pep talk was what he needed to hear.

We then walk inside to sit at the table, and it looks like Steven has already gotten here. I approach him to say hello. "Hayward!" he cuts me off before I can talk. I am nervous as to what he is going to say to me. After all, it was known that him and Alistair were close. I just recently took his mentor from him. He keeps talking, "Hayward, I want you to know something before we start . . . He was a good man . . . my king . . . he was just afraid of the future." They are hard words to hear because I believe them to be true. I just wish there could have been a way that Alistair would have seen the future that I see for Native's Point. "And another thing," he says, "I am truly sorry . . . We had reasons to think Samuel would cause trouble for us. Adonjay was a flawed man to say the least. But you . . . we judged you without knowing anything about you. I vow I will not make that mistake again."

"I know," I tell him, looking at the guilt in his face. "I look forward to seeing you make Alistair proud with how you handle Leonkam." I give him a smile as I take my seat. There is no need to dwell on the past . . . we can only look forward.

We wait until Queen May comes in, looking beautiful as ever. She smiles at me as she sits.

"Well, let's get started," King Timothy says, taking the floor.

We all talk and come to agreements of peace. This group is young and eager to work together to change this land to a great, safe place to live. A place where we stand together and are unable to fall to outside threats.

Once the meeting is over, I try to catch May before her wagon rides off. "May!" I yell, to get her to notice me.

"I was hoping you would come to talk to me before I took off," she says back to me. I look into her eyes and see determination to change this war for the better. "How are you?" I ask her.

"I have been settling into my role as queen well . . . there is much to do and well . . . the kingdom is a lot different without Samuel . . . I know it had to be done, but it does not make the loss of a friend any easier, I am sad to say." I wish I could have talked Samuel back to the light as well. Even after all he did. For May's sake. She is clearly still grieving her childhood friend.

"I am sure it's hard, I am sorry." I give her my condolences. She doesn't say anything. I am sure she just doesn't have the words to talk about the loss. Still, just looking in her eyes . . . it's like I can feel her emotions. I don't know if she can feel mine, but I have felt like she seems to understand me from the day I first met her in Leonkam. "May, I wanted to tell you . . ." I say to her. Her expression changes to one of curiosity.

"I just wanted to say, I hope we meet again soon . . . and that I know you're going to do great things in Autem," I tell her.

"Oh. Is that all you wanted to say?" she says back to me. "Thank you, Richard . . . for everything. I too hope we see each other again soon. Farwell, Hayward," she says before she rides off.

It's true I do have feelings for her, but how could it ever work? Right now, I am meant to be in Gresham, helping Timothy, and she is meant to be Queen in Autem . . . she deserves that much. I would just set her off course. Still, a part of me hopes, maybe one day, things will be different in our lives.

We ride back to Gresham, and I have plenty of time to think about how crazy this time in my life has been. I think of my father, as I have much in the last days. "Father, I know you're above me now. I hope you know how much I thank you for helping me be the man I am today. Without you in my life, I would have never been able to handle this war as well as I did," I think to myself.

We arrive at the stable of Gresham and Grace is there to meet us. "Safe travels, I hope?" she asks.

"Very much so. We came to agree on peace. Hopefully now our land will not see bloodshed again," I tell her.

"Good. Even if I have to go back to working at the stables because there are no men to treat medically, I would say that's a fair trade," she says.

"Not to worry, I am sure there will still be plenty of kids needing you to wrap their scrapes," I say back to her.

She smiles at me. "Yes, I would say so. Anyway, I have to go, Richard Hayward, but I do hope you won't be a stranger." She says to me, with charm. I watch her walk away and I think Gresham has some pretty great people as well. People I can trust like Grace and my cousin Timothy. Better days are coming, and I am happy to be with the people around me to work together to keep Native's Point safe!

END

www.ingramcontent.com/pod-product-compliance
Lightning Source LLC
LaVergne TN
LVHW051630080426
835511LV00016B/2269